William Sanday

The Oracles of God

Fourth Edition

William Sanday

The Oracles of God
Fourth Edition

ISBN/EAN: 9783337365646

Printed in Europe, USA, Canada, Australia, Japan

Cover: Foto ©Lupo / pixelio.de

More available books at **www.hansebooks.com**

The Oracles of God,

NINE LECTURES

ON THE

NATURE AND EXTENT OF BIBLICAL INSPIRATION

AND ON THE

SPECIAL SIGNIFICANCE OF THE OLD TESTAMENT
SCRIPTURES AT THE PRESENT TIME

𝔚𝔦𝔱𝔥 𝔗𝔴𝔬 𝔄𝔭𝔭𝔢𝔫𝔡𝔦𝔠𝔢𝔰

BY

W. SANDAY, M.A., D.D., LL.D.

DEAN IRELAND'S PROFESSOR OF EXEGESIS;

FELLOW OF EXETER COLLEGE; OXFORD PREACHER AT WHITEHALL

FOURTH EDITION

LONDON
LONGMANS, GREEN AND CO.
AND NEW YORK: 15 EAST 16TH STREET

1892

Oxford

HORACE HART, PRINTER TO THE UNIVERSITY

TO

MY FRIENDS AND COLLEAGUES

Samuel Rolles Driver   Thomas Kelly Cheyne

David Samuel Margoliouth

THIS LITTLE BOOK IS AFFECTIONATELY DEDICATED

IN GRATEFUL REMEMBRANCE

OF ALL THAT I OWE TO THEM IN THE PAST

AND IN CONFIDENT HOPE OF MORE

WHICH NOT ONLY I BUT MANY OTHERS WILL OWE TO THEM

IN THE FUTURE

Hoc erit pactum, quod feriam cum domo Israel post dies illos, dicit Dominus : Dabo legem meam in visceribus eorum, et in corde eorum scribam eam : et ero eis in Deum, et ipsi erunt mihi in populum.

PREFACE.

THE duty of the Theological Professor appears to be twofold : on the one hand to advance by all the means in his power the detailed study of the subject committed to him, and on the other to do what he can to help the public mind to clear itself in times of difficulty and perplexity. It is with some reluctance and self-distrust that the writer of these pages has turned away for the moment from the first of these functions to take up the second. He does not know how far the thoughts which have been helpful to himself may be helpful also to others, and he does not know how far he may be able to state them acceptably. Still the call has seemed to come to him, and he has obeyed it to the best of his ability.

Of the lectures which follow, the first six were preached as a course at Whitehall on the mornings and afternoons of three successive Sundays (July 27, August 3 and 10), which, if report speaks true, may prove to be the last on which the Chapel was open. If that should be the case they would also mark the close of a line of University preachers which has included many illustrious names. The lectures were shortly afterwards repeated in Oxford to some of the students who came up in connexion with the movement for University Extension : a few alterations were made to adapt them to this second purpose, and it was then that the notes were added. The subject of Lecture VII had been originally dealt with in one of these notes, but it was felt that it required a fuller treatment. This, therefore, with Lecture VIII, may be taken as supplementary to the original series. Lecture IX was delivered to a different audience from the University pulpit at St. Mary's. It should be said perhaps that in the case of all the earlier discourses the audience was of a very changing character : this involved a certain amount of repetition which it was attempted to reduce to as narrow limits as possible.

The lectures contain partly what the author wished to say and partly what he was compelled to say as the necessary set-off on the other side. Our age needs above all something positive—not exactly, as it is sometimes urged, positive teaching, or dogma, for which it does not see the reasons, but positive *reasons*, few, simple, and fundamental, which it can apprehend for itself and on which it can take its stand. Such reasons, or some of them, it has been the author's earnest desire to supply; and if in the course of stating them he has had to put forward the negative side of the question, it is only because he was bound in candour not to give the one without the other. It will be very much in accordance with his wishes if those to whom this is superfluous will pass on at once to Lectures III or IV where the positive argument begins.

The question was often asked at the Extension Lectures what books could be recommended as giving expression to the changed views of things here contemplated. As a simple and popular survey of the ground it did not seem easy to name a better book than one which came into the author's hands just as the lectures were being delivered, *The Nature and Method of Revelation*, by Dr. G. P. Fisher, Professor of Ecclesiastical History in the University of Yale (New York, Scribners; London, Fisher Unwin). Rather less popular and more limited in its range, but full of weighty thought, is *The Chief End of Revelation*, by Dr. A. B. Bruce (London, Hodder). On a larger scale, going fully into the criticism of the Old Testament, it was not possible to mention anything in English, but two companion volumes had recently appeared by a writer of singular sobriety of judgment who in the truth-loving pursuit of science never lost sight of the interests of religion, the posthumously published *Einleitung in das Alte Testament* and *Alttestamentliche Theologie* of Dr. Eduard Riehm, sometime Professor at Halle. It is hoped, however, that the English reader may soon be more immediately provided for by the promised *Introduction to the Literature of the Old Testament* from the pen of Dr. Driver. A very comprehensive and constructive little work, written in an admirable spirit, by another Halle Professor, recently deceased, Schlottmann's *Kompendium der Biblischen Theologie des Alten und Neuen Testaments*, is being translated by the Rev. A. Robertson, Principal of Bishop Hatfield's Hall, Durham. Happily, although English books written from a standpoint similar to this are rare, for the central point of all we have an almost ideal treatment in Dr. Driver's *Isaiah* (Nisbet), backed as it is by Professor Cheyne's commentary.

It only remains to add that the author's old and tried friend, Dr. Plummer, has done him the kindness to look over the proofs and help him with his advice.

MARCHFIELD, OXFORD.
October 20, 1890.

PREFACE

TO THE SECOND EDITION.

IN sending out a second edition of his little book the author cannot refrain from expressing his sense of the pains which have been taken by many, if not quite by all, of those who differed from him as well as of those who agreed with him, to deal justly and more than justly with what he has written. He could not have wished for a better or more faithful reproduction of the leading features of his book than has been accorded to it in more quarters than he could have hoped for.

The one feature which he was himself most anxious to succeed in bringing out was the appeal to the consciousness of those who were chosen to be the bearers of Revelation (Lecture IV). The best evidence for the reality of that Revelation seemed to him to be the clear and strong conviction on the part of those who gave expression to it, that it was no invention of their own, but that it was put into their thoughts directly by God. This view is in fact exactly that which is stated by Luther in one of his most striking aphorisms.

'Melanchthon discoursing with Luther touching the prophets, who continually boast thus, "Thus saith the Lord," asked whether God, in person, spoke with them or no. Luther

replied: They were very holy, spiritual people, who seriously
contemplated upon holy and divine things; therefore God
spake with them in their consciences, which the prophets
held as sure and certain revelations.'—(*Table Talk*, DXLIX).

The great Reformer was a man of unguarded speech,
and laid himself open to criticisms which have been
meted out to him somewhat unsparingly of late; it
may be well therefore to note in passing, what quiet
thought, what genuine religious apprehension lay behind his vehement utterance. We are however rather
concerned with the substance of this particular saying,
which sums up better than the writer himself could
the gist of what he wished to say. He is the more
glad to have such an authority at his back, because it
is just this part of his argument which is taken up
and directly challenged by an able critic in the
Inquirer for Feb. 28, 1891.

'In the midst of this manifold imperfectness, it is difficult
to see where the alleged "inspiration" can come in, or what
has been the good of it. This divine quality does, however,
we are told, abundantly manifest and vindicate itself. It is
seen, first, in the fact that Moses, Isaiah, and other eminent
Biblical characters were pressed into their legislative or prophetic office against their own will, and therefore the impulse
which moved them came to them from without—or in other
words, was the product of the divine afflatus which we term
Inspiration. But then the passages relied upon to prove this
(in Exodus iii., Isaiah vi., Jerem. i., and others) may surely
be referred simply to the sacred writer's *style*, his vivid and
earnest manner of expressing the resolves of his own mind,
as suggested to him by the circumstances around him. As
for example, when Isaiah (xx.) says that the Lord told him
to walk *naked and barefoot three years for a sign and a
wonder upon Egypt*, or when Ezekiel (iii.) says that the Lord
commanded him to eat the roll of the book, and in another

place (iv.) to *take a tile* and portray upon it a siege of Jerusalem—are we to think that in such narratives as these (which are pretty numerous in the prophets) actual occurrences are recorded? Are they not simply the prophet's way of describing, pictorially and figuratively, his own thoughts and purposes? Clearly the latter is the only rational explanation.'

It will hardly be denied that if some of these symbolical acts are regarded as taking place in trance or vision (Isa. vi. 6 f., Ezek. iii. 1 f.) others are as clearly regarded as literally put into execution (Isa. xx. 2 f., Ezek. iv. 1 ff.; cf. 1 Kings xi. 29 ff., xx. 35 ff., xxii. 11, &c.). But the question is whether the prompting was really external to the prophet and really came from God as he supposed it to come. It need not be disputed that the particular form which the symbolism took was as much the product of the prophet's own mind as the words which he wrote came to him by natural processes; but unless we would explain away the language of the Bible altogether, we must needs believe that there was an impulse from above working through and guiding those processes. Certainly the biblical writers imagined themselves to be doing something more than using metaphors. We may think that they were mistaken, and to a materialist this is the only explanation possible, but if we once believe that there is a spiritual Being who does hold any sort of converse with the soul of man, then it becomes far more reasonable to take the prophets at their word. The alternative is to explain away not only these but a myriad other facts of human consciousness in like manner. And if that were done we might as well close the book of human thought altogether, and content ourselves with inscribing *Vanitas vanitatum* outside.

On one other crucial point a word should be added. In speaking of the *condescension* of the Son of God (p. 111), it is right that full stress should be laid on the voluntary nature of that condescension. Justice must be done to the strongly reflexive form of the Greek text in the passage on which it mainly turns: ἐκένωσεν ἑαυτόν, *He emptied Himself*—by no external compulsion but by that same free and gracious act by which He took our nature upon Him. One of the author's most scholarly correspondents reminds him of a passage with which he was not unfamiliar, though he had not thought of using it in this connexion. As far back as Irenaeus the necessity was seen for taking account of this side of the Incarnation. The phrase which he used was the *quiescence* of the Word (τὸ ἡσυχάζειν τοῦ Λόγου, *Adv. Haer.* iii. 19. 3). It was by means of this conception that Irenaeus explained the possibility that the Son of Man could undergo temptation; and His self-renunciation in matters of literary knowledge may well be placed in the same category.

In the present edition some errors of the press have been corrected, and a few verbal changes have been made chiefly in the Biblical quotations in cases where greater accuracy seemed desirable. The only addition is the valuable Note to Appendix I, for the substance of which the author is indebted to the kindness of Dr. Driver.

Easter, 1891.

CONTENTS.

I.

THE PRESENT DISQUIETUDE.

(Whitehall, July 27, 1890.)

HEBREWS i. 1, 2.

God, who at sundry times and in divers manners spake in time past unto the fathers by the Prophets, hath in these last days spoken unto us by His Son.

THERE is concentrated in these words a whole philosophy of revelation. They contain a summary view of the more special dealings of God with man. They embrace the age of patriarchs, prophets, and apostles, and they trace the course which the several revelations of God followed till they finally culminated in His Son.

Before we go more fully into the passage just a word should be said as to its exact meaning. This is apt to be obscured by the rendering with which we are most familiar. The free and beautiful rhythm of our old Bibles is gained at some cost of minute accuracy of expression, which is preserved in the stiffer and less living version adopted by the Revisers : *God having of old time spoken unto the fathers in the prophets by divers portions and in divers manners,*

B

hath at the end of these days spoken unto us in His Son (more strictly still *in One who is Son*) [1].

By many portions and in many manners is the characteristic phrase which is chosen to describe the methods of God's Spirit up to that final epoch inaugurated by the coming of the Son. It would probably be true to say that the fitness of these words has never been appreciated so fully as it is now. Let us ask ourselves what they mean.

They mean, first, that the revelation of God to man has not been made all at once. It has been a long process and a gradual process; a process broken up into parts and those parts all fitting into each other, so as to form not merely a continuous chain but an articulated whole. Mahometanism has but a single prophet. Its sacred book is the work of one, man. Its doctrines were all proclaimed at one time. Its Theology was built up from beginning to end in the course of a single life. It had no period of preparation. It came into the world as an adult system ; at least its maturity was reached so rapidly that it might be described as adult. I am not of course speaking of Mahometanism as a historical phenomenon. Historically it has its antecedents, and those antecedents can be explained and traced ; but as a prophet Mahomet had no precursors. He brought his own credentials ; he delivered his own message ; he left

---

[1] The preposition cannot rightly be explained as merely instrumental: cf. Rom. i. 19, Gal. i. 16.

that message in a form which he intended to be final, and to need no supplementing by others.

In all these respects the faith of Christ and that of Mahomet stand in marked contrast. Mahomet indeed had Christianity and Judaism to build upon, or he would never have reached the height that he did. He himself to some extent recognised his obligations. But when we think of Mahometanism, we think of a religion promulgated once for all as a whole. And the difference when we turn to our own Bibles helps us to realize what is meant by *divers portions*.

Then again, secondly, Christianity, has also been revealed in *divers manners*. There may be unity beneath the diversity, but still the result is diverse. *All these worketh the self-same Spirit, dividing to every man severally as He will.* Our Christian revelation is expressed through the medium of many individualities. Paul is one ; Apollos is another ; Cephas is distinct from both, and yet more James. The New Testament is full of different types and shades of teaching. And if the New Testament, quite as much the Old. There we have lawgiver, historian, psalmist, prophet ; and not only ' prophet ' but ' prophets,' not only ' psalmist ' but ' psalmists,' not only ' historian ' but ' historians.' How clearly here again do some of the types stand before us ! How different is Jeremiah from Isaiah, Amos from Hosea, Micah from Ezekiel !

And if these distinctions and idiosyncrasies appear in the authors whom we know, may we not expect to find them equally in the authors whom we do not know, in the anonymous composers of psalms or narratives? As a matter of fact we do find them; and the labours of successive generations of scholars have succeeded in discriminating some of them with great nicety.

Much might be said about this, and something may perhaps be said at some future time, but I do not wish at present to raise any difference of opinion. So far I believe that I shall have carried all my hearers with me. I have in fact merely paraphrased —and that in the most general terms—the words of my text. It is when we leave general terms that divergence begins. *God spake of old time to the fathers in the prophets, by divers portions and in divers manners.* In other words, God revealed Himself through that long period of time which preceded the coming of Christ, through His prophets in ways which were partial and differing in individuals though coalescing together so as to form a whole.

Still I do not think that there will be any disagreement with this. It is only when we come to close quarters and ask, *in what sense* 'God spake,' in what sense He revealed Himself, to what precise extent the revelations given by Him were partial, to what precise extent the individuality of the messenger entered into his message, that differences of opinion will arise.

And here I know that I am beginning to tread upon dangerous, because sacred, ground. I am beginning to touch on matters in which deep feelings are involved. And I must beware, or do my best to beware, of making sad the heart of the righteous whom the Lord hath not made sad.

It cannot be denied that there is not a little disquietude and anxiety in the air, and that especially amongst good people. They are concerned at opinions which have been expressed upon a point which I am now approaching. They have recently become aware—more fully aware than they were before—of a considerable change of front among scholars and thoughtful men in regard primarily to the Old Testament, but we might add also to the New. And the form which this has taken is such as to excite uneasiness and apprehension.

This uneasy feeling is not lessened by the fact that the expressions of opinion by which it has been excited have not had anything of the nature of an attack. They have not come from the Extreme Left or from the destructive party in ecclesiastical politics and theology, but they have come from men of known weight and sobriety of judgment, from men of strong, Christian convictions, who it is felt would not lightly disturb the same convictions in others, men, too, of learning, who do not speak without knowing what they say.

It is not mine to interpose with authority in these matters. In these days it is necessary for every one who would do sound and permanent work to choose some definite line. And the line which I have chosen stretches forwards from the New Testament rather than backwards. In regard to the Old Testament I can only look on from outside. But at the same time one who holds a responsible position must do his best to ascertain which way things are tending : he must not let any considerable change in theology come upon him unprepared : he must consider beforehand how it is likely to affect himself and to affect others, especially those who come under his charge. And it is from that point of view that the remarks which I am about to make in this and in succeeding sermons will be offered.

I shall abstain from expressing any opinion as to the extent to which the conclusions involved have been proved. In regard to this there may be not a few here who will be as well able to form a judgment as I am. I, like them, must be content to take a great deal upon trust. The only advantage I can claim is perhaps a rather fuller acquaintance with foreign work as well as with English, and with the general balance of opinion abroad as well as at home. I have also the advantage that some of those engaged in these studies are personal friends of my own, and to their singleness of mind and earnest religious purpose, as well as to their thorough competence to deal with questions of so much importance, I must needs bear testimony.

The question as to which I said that there was a change of front is as to the nature of God's revelation of Himself in the Bible, and especially in the Old Testament, or more accurately as to the nature of the methods by which that revelation has been conveyed. There is no change at all in respect to the Divine attributes revealed in the Old Testament; there is no change as to the lessons of human duty to be derived from it; no change as to the general conclusion that the Old Testament points forward prophetically to Christ, though there may be some change in the interpretation of particular prophecies: but there is a change in regard to the conception of the Old Testament itself as the vehicle of revelation.

I will endeavour the next time we meet to state more precisely in what this change consists. For the present I will content myself with attempting to answer the preliminary question, *why* there should be any such change. All, no doubt, will not admit the reasons. The student of the subject must form his own opinion as to how far they are adequate. I simply state the fact that they exist.

The reasons are partly external and partly internal.

Partly they turn upon the discovery or extended use of new material, and partly they depend upon the closer analysis of the sacred texts.

The Old Testament has not been unaffected by the explorations which have been going on so actively in the East for the last half century. In Egypt, Palestine, Assyria, and Babylonia much has been done. The enterprise of English societies has surveyed and mapped a great part of the Holy Land, and has unearthed the buried monuments of the ancient Egyptian civilization. In both these tasks French and German *savants* have also been busy. Many of the sculptures which adorned the Assyrian palaces had before this found their way through private energy to the British Museum or the Louvre. Whole libraries of the baked brick tablets which served for books have been disinterred from the mounds in which they lay, and are being deciphered and published. A whole people, the Hittites, have been, as it were, resuscitated from their grave, though as yet our knowledge of them is but slight.

In many respects the result of these discoveries has been to confirm the truth of the Old Testament history—in many, but not quite in all.

An instructive example is supplied by the chronology. Both the Assyrian and the Babylonian chronologies rest on a very secure basis. They can be traced up to authorities which are either contemporary or nearly contemporary. And they are further confirmed by the mention of astronomical phenomena, such as eclipses, which have been verified by modern calculations. Now although these chronologies present a great deal of approximate agreement with the Books of Kings there are some not unimportant differences [1].

[1] The state of the case is this. For the Assyrian chronology we have what are called the 'Eponymous lists,' that is lists of certain officials after whom the years were reckoned, just as at Rome they were reckoned after the consuls. These lists exist in two forms, a shorter which gives the names only, and a longer which adds brief notes of contemporary events. The first extends from 893-666 B.C., the second only from 817-728 B.C. or a little further. In addition to the lists there are also inscriptions of the different kings. For the later Babylonian history we have the so-called Ptolemaean Canon. Ptolemy is the celebrated geographer and astronomer who lived at Alexandria in the second century A.D. He has preserved for us a list, originally carried from Babylonia to Egypt, of the Babylonian kings from Nabonassar in 747 downwards. The accuracy of this list is doubly vouched for, by coincidences with the Assyrian records and also by the mention of eclipses.

The Assyrian and the Biblical data agree exactly in assigning the Fall of Samaria to the year 722 B.C., but some correction is required of the statement in 2 Kings xviii. 10 that this event took place in the sixth year of King Hezekiah. Sennacherib's invasion, which three verses lower is assigned to the fourteenth year of the same king, did not really take place until after the year 702. This point I believe is well made out; and it appears to be also necessary to shorten the reigns of Uzziah, which has fifty-two years assigned to it in 2 Kings xv. 2, and of Manasseh, which is reckoned fifty-five years in 2 Kings xxi. 1. I take these points of chronology as involving a clear and definite issue, and because a strong case can be made out for the non-Biblical authorities in regard to them. (See Riehm, *Einleitung*, i. 464 ff.; Rösch in Herzog, xvii. 474 ff. ed. 2; Schrader, *Keilinschiften*, &c. p. 292 ff.) Another instance

Of another kind was the discovery of the tablets which contain Babylonian versions of the Creation and of the Flood. With all their inferiority, the resemblance of these to the corresponding Biblical stories was striking and needed to be accounted for[1].

of the same kind, in which the Bible is at variance with a contemporary monument, is in regard to the revolt of Moab from Israel which, according to 2 Kings i. 1, iii. 5, took place *after*, but according to the Moabite stone *before* the death of Ahab (see Driver, *Notes on Heb. Text of the Books of Samuel*, p. lxxxviii f.).

[1] The most searching examination of the Babylonian versions will probably be found in Jensen, *Die Kosmologie der Babylonier*, Strassburg, 1890. The English reader should consult especially an article by Dr. Driver in the *Expositor* for January, 1886. It would seem that traditions in respect to the Creation and the Flood were originally the common property of the Semitic races, developed by each in accordance with the genius of its religion. We shall see later (Lecture V.) that they were not of a kind to be referred directly to Revelation; at the same time in the Hebrew version the influence of the Spirit of Revelation is clearly visible, not on the side which belongs of right to science, but in all that concerns the nature and relations of God and man. Even from the point of view of science, when allowance is made for the simple mode of presentation which alone was possible when the early chapters of Genesis were written, we may see an approximation to the truth which the believer in Providence will easily refer to its origin: but we must be careful not to exaggerate the extent of this approximation. The history of science reveals plainly that God has permitted the evolution of true ideas on scientific subjects to be entangled in a mass of fantastic error. In the Biblical account this appears to be reduced to something like a minimum. More than this we cannot safely say. [I am glad to be able to refer to an article by the Dean of Peterborough in the *Expositor* for October, 1890. He quotes an authority no less unprejudiced than Haeckel as affirming that 'from Moses, who died about 1480 B.C., down to Linnaeus, who was born 1707 A.D., there has been no history of creation to be compared to the Biblical' (p. 243).]

By the side of this and of more far-reaching significance are the results obtained—or at least thought
to be obtained—from the critical investigation of the
Bible itself. The last hundred years have been a
time of great activity, in which literary problems of
all kinds have had much attention paid to them.
The Bible also is a literature, and it was inevitable
that the same methods which had been applied to
other literatures should be applied also to it [1]. It

[1] In regard to the analytic criticism of the Old Testament I may
remark that there is for the most part in England a very imperfect idea
of the immense mass of literature and of close detailed study dealing
with it. The most prominent problem relates to the composition of
the Pentateuch. The systematic treatment of this may be said to date
from the French Court-physician Astruc, whose work, under the title
*Conjectures sur les Mémoires originaux, dont il paroit, que Moyse s'est
servi pour composer le livre de Genèse,* appeared at Brussels in 1753.
From that time onwards, but especially in the last fifty years, an almost
incessant stream of publications upon the subject has come out, most
of them dealing with the subject at first hand and with great minute-
ness and care. A very significant fact was the conversion of the veteran
Delitzsch, who died on March 4th of this year at the age of nearly
seventy-seven, substantially to the new views. A man of extraordinary
learning and of deep piety, he had all his life long contended for the
Mosaic authorship of the Pentateuch, until first, in two preliminary essays
published in 1880 and 1882, and then in the fifth edition of his Com-
méntary on Genesis, published in 1887, he threw over this, and without
admitting any change in his religious convictions he practically went
over to the other side. We must not lose sight either of the enormous
amount of labour expended on this subject, or of the very considerable
extent of agreement which has been reached upon it on the Continent.
It is agreed on all hands that the Pentateuch is formed by the dovetail-
ing together of different documents; it is agreed by the great mass of

has been approached by friends and approached by enemies, approached by religious minds and approached by others the primary interest of which was not religious. What then? Is not the Bible capable of satisfying all this manifold curiosity? The landowner who holds his property by long and lineal descent does not mind having his title deeds examined. And we with eighteen centuries of Christian history behind us—with eighteen centuries, nay, with more than twice eighteen centuries in which the finger of God has been visibly manifest ordering and guiding the course of events down to this present— why should we take alarm? why should we expect that anything but good should issue from the process, in the future more than in the past?

enquirers that nearly all of these documents in their present shape are not earlier than the time of the Kings. The points most debated are (1) how far the traditions embodied in these documents go back ultimately to Moses, and (2) whether a particular document, the so-called Priestly Code, is earlier or later than the Exile. An average view of the results obtained for the Book of Genesis is conveniently presented in a work by two Tübingen Professors, Kautzsch and Socin, who have printed the text in different types corresponding to the different documents (*Die Genesis mit äusserer Unterscheidung der Quellenschriften*, Freiburg i. B., 1888). Similar problems arise in respect to the historical books. The other most prominent questions are the assignment of large parts of the Book of Isaiah and of the last six chapters of Zechariah to writers other than the authors of the main body of the book—in the case of Isaiah later, and in the case of Zechariah earlier ; and the dates of the composition of many parts of the Psalter and the Books of Joel, Jonah, Job, Ecclesiastes and Daniel.

Whatever happens, the foundation of God stands sure, and must stand sure. There is one assumption from which we can start with confidence. All sound knowledge the Christian faith can assimilate. If there is anything which it cannot assimilate, that we may firmly believe is not sound. Of course time is needed before we can ascertain what will stand the test and what will not—time and a calm unruffled temper, not easily moved by the swayings to and fro of the moment.

The best sign of which I am aware is the gradual growth of this temper. Not many years have passed since the cry was wont to be, *He that is not with us is against us.* Everything which did not at once fall in with preconceived ideas was treated as an 'attack.' Hostility and bitterness on one side were met by hostility and bitterness on the other. Men were driven with or against their will into two great opposing camps. It did not seem possible to be critical and yet reverent, devout and yet candid. Now, I trust, our faith is stronger. We do not see an enemy in every bush. We do not think it necessary to meet every question that arises with a peremptory *yes* or *no.* We are able to wait and look around and take our bearings without being hurried or disturbed. Such at least seems to me to be the attitude of that younger generation which is now coming to the front in these matters. It is, to my mind, an attitude which is not only a hopeful one, but the only attitude which really becomes a Christian.

I would fain, if I may, make some small contribution to the question of the hour. I propose this afternoon and on succeeding Sundays to do what I can to estimate the effect upon a Christian's faith of the changes which seem to be in progress. There must be in this an element of anticipation. I do not say that all that I may regard as possible is as yet completely proved. It may perhaps never be proved. If that is so our course is plain. We only have to remain where we are. But it is right for us to keep in view contingencies which will seem to some at least more or less probable. And I hope that I may be able to show that if those contingencies should be realized, there is not only no reason for despair— despair is a word which should not cross (I do not say the lips but) even the thought of a Christian—but that they may leave his faith stronger, richer, deeper than it was before. There may be loss as well as gain ; and yet I cannot but think that the gain will be found to overbalance the loss, and that all things —even the progress of criticism—still work together for good to those who love the Lord Jesus Christ in sincerity.

II.

THE HUMAN ELEMENT IN THE BIBLE.

(Whitehall, July 27, 1890.)

2 CORINTHIANS iv. 7.

We have this treasure in earthen vessels.

LET me take up the subject proposed this morning by endeavouring to state, in as summary a form as possible, the main points in that change of which I spoke as coming over the conception which many good and instructed Christian men hold of the Bible.

It has for a long time been distinctly recognised that there is a human as well as a divine element in the Book by which God has been pleased to convey the revelation of Himself to us. However much we may feel that the Holy Spirit itself is present in that Book, and speaks to us through its pages, there can be no question that it speaks through human media. It was the hand of man which held the pen. The words written down were human words. They are governed by the ordinary laws of language; and the forms of expression which they assume are not always perfect as men count perfection.

This we may start with, that there is a human element even in the Bible; and the tendency of the last 50 or 100 years of investigation is to make it appear that this human element is larger than had been supposed. The freedom of the human agents made use of in the Bible was less restricted than those who argued from an antecedent view of what was to be expected in a Divine revelation would have imagined it to be.

That is the first point; but the second, which seems to me to be equally clear, is that, in spite of the enlarged scope which is thus given to human thought and human action, the Divine element which lies behind it is not less real and not less Divine.

The third point is that we make a mistake in attempting to draw a hard and fast line between the two elements. The part which comes from man and the part which comes from God run into and blend with each other. We think of them best not as acting separately but as acting together. And this intimate or organic union only serves to bring home the message which God has condescended to speak to man with greater force and greater reality.

Lastly, I think it will be seen that the application which we in turn make of that message may need to be somewhat modified. We may find our view of the motive forces in religion somewhat altered. I do not think for a moment that we shall find them less powerful or less effective than they have been.

Bear with me if I try now and next week to explain in more detail the nature of these conclusions—not in any spirit of wanton innovation, but only to help those who find themselves face to face with new conditions which they do not feel able simply to put aside and ignore. And permit me to ask that no one will listen to the negative side of what I have to say without also listening to the positive side. The function of the teacher in these days is like the function of the prophet of old : he is not called upon only *to break down and to overthrow*, but *to build and to plant*[1].

This applies especially to my present duty this afternoon. I must begin by seeming at least to contend for an encroachment of the human element upon the Divine. If I do so, let me beg of those who are willing to pay any attention to this part of what I have to say, also to give a hearing to what seems to me to be the complementary or counterbalancing truth, the affirmation which I shall have to make next of the undiminished—nay, the heightened—reality of the Divine element which lies behind and gives an impulse to the human. I cannot claim

[1] Jeremiah i. 10.

C

to be heard on either side of the argument, but
I may ask that one may not be taken without the
other.

To assume then this ungracious and unwelcome
but I fear necessary task, I must first point out how
it is probably true that the human element in. the
Scriptures is larger than many good people now, and
nearly all good people not long ago, supposed it
to be.

Let us take a glance at the history of the doctrine
of Inspiration. The writers and teachers of the early
Church doubtless held a high view of it, but it was
not by any means a mechanical view. They would
not have hesitated to admit what we might call slips
of the pen[1]. Origen went further in admitting positive

---

[1] Take for instance the patristic comments upon Matt. xxvii. 9, where
a saying which really belongs to Zechariah is attributed to Jeremiah.
Origen thinks that there has either been some error in writing by which
Jeremiah is put for Zechariah, or else that the passage might be found
among the apocryphal works of Jeremiah. St. Augustine mentions the
omission in some MSS. of the name Jeremiah, so that the sentence runs
through the prophet only, and not *through Jeremiah the prophet.*
He will not lay stress on this because the word is found both in the
majority of Latin MSS. and also in the Greek text. He is rather inclined to think that the name *Jeremiah* occurred to St. Matthew
instead of *Zechariah*, and that he would have corrected it if he had not
remembered that the Spirit might have determined him to write thus
in order to bring out that all the prophets really said the same thing.
St. Jerome says roundly that there is a mistake here as in Matt. xiii. 35
(*videtis ergo quia et hic error fuit sicut ibi*). See the passages quoted in
Tischendorf *ad loc.*

error in the literal statements if not in the deeper sense of Scripture. If the language of St. Augustine as to the composition of the Gospels were to be pressed, he, too, would be committed to views which implied considerable freedom of handling [1].

At the Reformation we know with what freedom Luther spoke upon the subject. We know how he singled out a particular branch of Christian doctrine —a Gospel within the Gospel—and how applying this as a test to the different parts of the Bible he put a high or a low value upon them according to the degree in which it was embodied, venturing even to call one Epistle an *epistle of straw*, because that for which he looked was not to be found there.

In the latitude which he thus allowed himself, Luther was not imitated by his followers. On the contrary, it was really the Reformation which led to the predominance of the stricter view. It was a leading principle of the Reformation to throw wholly upon the Bible the weight of authority which had hitherto been shared by it with tradition. *The Bible, and the*

---

[1] Speaking of the discrepancies in the Gospels, Origen says that 'if one were to set them all forth then would he turn dizzy, and either desist from trying to establish all the Gospels in very truth, and attach himself to one, ... or, admitting the four, grant that the truth does not lie in their corporeal forms' (ἐν τοῖς σωματικοῖς χαρακτῆρσι: *Comm. in Joan.* x. 2, quoted by Westcott, *Introd.* p. 419, ed. 3). St. Augustine describes the Second Gospel as an 'epitome' of the First, in which case the Evangelist could not have kept to his text very closely.

Bible only, became the watchword of the Reformed Churches. Hence we cannot be surprised if its authority was most jealously safeguarded. The one broad foundation on which the whole of Christianity seemed to rest must needs be without flaw.

The rigid theory which thus came in led to some palpable exaggerations. As the study of Hebrew revived, the scholars of the sixteenth and seventeenth centuries began to win back little by little the knowledge which had been lost. Now-a-days every one knows that ancient Hebrew—the Hebrew of the Old Testament—was written purely in consonants without vowels. The vowels were added by a group of diligent Jewish scribes and students of the Scriptures in the sixth and seventh centuries after Christ. This was first made out by a French professor, Louis Cappel or Cappellus, in the Calvinistic Academy of Saumur[1]. The book was quietly received, until in 1648 a sharp attack was made upon it by one of the most learned Hebraists of his day, the younger Buxtorf; and a controversy arose in which the set of opinion throughout the Reformed Churches was so strong that a later work by Cappellus[2] could only be

[1] *Arcanum punctationis revelatum*, published at Leyden anonymously, under the care of Erpenius, in 1624.

[2] This was the *Critica Sacra* published at Paris in 1650. Riehm (*Einleitung*, p. 21) does not appear to be strictly correct in saying that the son, Jean Cappel, 'found himself compelled, after his father's death, to become a Roman Catholic in order to publish the book.' He had joined the Roman Church some time previously in spite of his father's

published by the help of his son, who had joined the
Church of Rome. It was in that Church that the
view which is now universally held to be the right
one found its ablest advocates. The writer indeed
who laid the foundation of Old and New Testament criticism was a member of that Church—the
Oratorian Richard Simon[1]. So far did opinion go
upon the other side that in one of the Swiss formularies, dated 1675, it is expressly laid down that
not only the consonants but the vowel-points of the
Hebrew text were divinely inspired[2].

The question could not rest here. It soon came
to be understood that more was involved than the
vowel-points. The less-instructed sort of Protestants
pinned their faith to the versions which every man
was now able to read in his own tongue. But
they could not help admitting that an appeal lay
beyond them to the originals[3]. It could not be

remonstrances; and the father did not die until 1658, so that he must
have been aware of the steps his son was taking.

[1] *Histoire Critique du Vieux Testament*, 1685; *Histoire Critique du
Text du N. T.* (1689), *des Versions* (1690), *des principaux Commenta-
teurs* (1693).

[2] *Consensus Ecclesiarum Helveticarum Can. II.: Hebraicus Vet.
Test. codex . . . tum quoad consonas tum quoad vocalia sive puncta ipsa
sive punctorum saltem potestatem . . .* θεόπνευστος, &c. Quoted by
Riehm, *Einl.* p. 22.

[3] In the Westminster Assembly of Divines, in which as a member of
Parliament he had a right to sit and debate, 'Mr. Selden spake admirably
and confuted divers of them in their own learning. And sometimes

maintained that all these versions, the origin of which was known and which often differed widely from each other, enjoyed any special inspiration. But if so, where was it that inspiration really resided? What guarantee was there that the Greek and Hebrew texts from which those versions were made truly and accurately represented that which had really proceeded from the sacred writers? When men began to think and to enquire they would have no difficulty in tracing the origin of these Greek and Hebrew texts. They too were made by certain known scholars from certain known MSS., but when these MSS. came to be compared with others which lay upon the shelves of the European libraries, there was found to be a great diversity among them. Further, it was found in regard to the Greek of the New Testament that, to speak roughly, the older a MS. was the more widely it differed from the common printed copies. But there was a presumption at least that these older copies, as they were nearer to the originals, so also would represent them more faithfully. So arose by degrees the science of Textual Criticism, which attempts by comparing together the different MSS. and other authorities

when they had cited a text of Scripture to prove their assertion, he would tell them *perhaps in your little Pocket Bibles with gilt leaves* (which they would often pull out and read) *the Translation may be thus, but the* Greek *or the* Hebrew *signifies thus and thus*; and so would totally silence them.' Whitelocke, *Memorials*, p. 71, ed. 1732.

to get at the truth of what was originally written. The method by which this is done has become much more elaborate and systematic, but even yet a complete consent has not been reached ; and although the limits of possible error are not really very wide, and although the great mass of the Greek text is not open to question, still a residue even yet remains about which we cannot be absolutely certain that we have the actual words of the Apostolic writers before us.

The question as to the Hebrew text of the Old Testament seems easier, but is in reality more difficult than that as to the Greek text of the New [1]. There is not indeed the same amount of difference between the MSS., though the oldest of these is younger by several centuries than the oldest MSS. of the New Testament. In other ways it is possible to trace back the Hebrew text up to and even beyond the time at which the vowel-points came to be attached to it. From the end of the fourth century of the Christian era onwards we may say that the care bestowed upon the copying of the Old Testament was so great that no important

[1] 'The majority of Hebrew MSS. are of the twelfth to the sixteenth centuries. Very few are earlier : the earliest of which the date is known with certainty being the MS. of the later Prophets, now at St. Petersburg, which bears a date = A.D. 916 ' (Driver's *Notes on Heb. Text of the Books of Samuel*, p. xxxvi). The oldest MSS. of N. T. are assigned to the fourth century.

variation was possible. It is further back still that the real problem begins. We possess, as it happens, versions of the Old Testament made some before and some not very long after the Christian era. These versions make it clear that at that earlier date there was a much larger amount of diversity. And it is behind this that the critic has to penetrate ; so that his task is even more difficult than that which lies before the critic of the New Testament, and at the present stage the results obtained are even less certain.

Such is the state of the case on one line of investigation, the investigation of the text. On other lines the course which events have taken has been very similar. At one time it was held, in pursuance of the same view of doctrine which we have been hitherto considering, that the language of the New Testament writers must needs be perfect, and their grammar faultless [1]. Now it is distinctly recognised that this is far from the fact ; that the language of the New Testament writers, though an excellent instrument in its way, contains not only many Hebraisms, but many an idiom which belongs to popular speech and by no means conforms to the standards of literary correctness.

Again, on more important ground it is well known

---

[1] The most extreme of the Purists were Pfochen (1629), Musaeus (1641, 1642), Georgi (1732, 1733), and Schwarz (1736). See Winer's *Grammar*, pp. 13-15 (i. 1. § 1) E. T.

what a conflict has long been maintained between the Bible and Natural Science. The names of Galileo, Newton, Darwin recall to us conspicuous instances in which the Bible has been invoked to check the course of free enquiry, and, as we can now see, wrongly invoked. It is coming to be agreed among thinking men that the Bible was never meant to teach science, and that the Biblical writers simply shared the scientific beliefs of their own day and expressed themselves in the language which was currently used all around them. . .

What I have been describing so far is a state of opinion which has been very generally reached, and in regard to which there is little room left for sharp antagonism. To some extent, as regards at least the uncertainty of Greek and Hebrew readings, it has found expression in a public document like the Revised Version. But having reached this point the question will, of necessity, force itself upon some minds: having gone so far, is there not room to go still further? The Bible has not been exempted from the fate of other books: it has been copied, and in the process of copying its text has been corrupted: it has been transmitted across centuries of declining knowledge: it has passed through the hands of scribes who were both ignorant and careless, and whose ignorance and carelessness have hardly done so much mischief as well-intentioned but unfortunate attempts at correction [1]. Neither again were the Biblical writers exempted from some at least of the general characteristics of their contemporaries: they shared the literary peculiarities of men of their own nationality and station: they were not supernaturally raised above the level of knowledge to which their contemporaries had attained in matters of science. Even in the things of religion it is becoming every day clearer that there is a growth and progression running through the New Testament as well as the Old. No one generation reached the limits of truth all at once: there was a gradual withdrawing of the veil *at different times and in different portions.*

It may be asked then, independently of any critical enquiries, where can we draw the line and say *Hitherto and no further?* We admit that the Bible has shared the fate of other books in its subsequent history. May it not also have shared the fate of other books in the circumstances of its origin? We admit that the writers spoke and wrote in the language of their contemporaries, with many at least of the same faults of style and diction, with some

---

[1] 'The Syrian text' (i.e. the text substantially current in the later MSS. and in the older printed editions, the original of the so-called Textus Receptus) 'must in fact be the result of a recension in the proper sense of the word, a work of attempted criticism, performed deliberately by editors and not merely by scribes' (Westcott and Hort, *Introduction,* p. 133).

at least of the same defects of knowledge. But if
with some, why not also with others? They were
not perfectly acquainted with the facts of science :
is it certain that they would be more perfectly
acquainted with the facts of history? In the secular
writings of antiquity there are many phenomena
which are not in exact accordance with the literary
practice of our own day. A later writer will incor-
porate the work of an older writer often with but
slight alteration. The annals that are transmitted
from age to age receive gradual accretions in their
course, and there is often no external mark to show
where the older matter ends and the new begins.
Institutions which are well established in one age
are assumed to go back to an earlier date than can
really be claimed for them. Certain great names
stand out in the history round which stray documents
and stray incidents appear to crystallize. When a
group of writings is collected together the name
which stands at the head of the group is held to
cover every member of it. And in like manner
laws and customs which grow up by slow degrees
are referred to some one great lawgiver who was
the first to formulate the leading provisions of the
code with which they are associated. There is no
deception about it. It is the same sort of process
that we see going on every day where oral tradition
is at work. Wherever some notable character has

passed over the stage, in aftertime things come to be set down to him with which he has no real connexion. We must throw ourselves back into an age when writing is the exception and hearsay the rule. There comes a time when regular histories are written, but before that tradition has been at work moulding and combining the facts which history records.

Processes like these have gone on in all the ancient literatures which have been preserved to us. Can we say that the literature of Israel is an exception? Is there reason to think that that alone has had an immunity from conditions which are elsewhere universal? Some of the best and most competent judges tell us that it is not so. They tell us that in the Old Testament—yes, and in the New Testament too—there are books which are composite in their origin, which were not written as we have them all at once, but which were put together at sundry times and in divers manners, one document here and another document there, welded together into a single whole, but not so welded that all traces of the combination are obliterated. They tell us that there are aggregates of writings which pass under names which of right belong only to a part of them. They tell us that laws and customs of a later date are sometimes attributed to an earlier; that not all the historical statements rest upon contemporary record, but that some of them have passed through a stage—longer or shorter—of tradition, before they were committed to writing.

This we are told, and that not lightly or conjecturally, but as a result of close examination. The body of proof is weighty and cannot easily be rejected. Why should it be rejected? The grounds, when we come to think of it, are mainly those of our own imagination. We do not think it likely that God would allow the revelation of Himself to be mixed up with such imperfect materials. But we are no good judges of what God would or would not do. *His ways are not as our ways.* Out of the imperfect He brings forth the perfect. It is so in the world of nature, and it is so in the world of grace. *We have our treasure in earthen vessels.* The vessels may be earthen, but the treasure which they contain is Divine. It is best for us not to trouble our minds with vain speculations as to what ought to be, but to take with thankfulness that which is. After all there are, as I hope to be able to show, two sides to the question. We can imagine the Bible in some of its accessories more perfect than it is— what we at least might think more perfect. But if it had been so it could never have been in such close contact with human nature. Its message could never have come home to us so fresh and warm as it does. As it is, it speaks to the heart, and it does so because, according to a fine saying in the Talmud, *it speaks in the tongue of the children of men.*

I hope to show, as I proceed, that none of the qualifications to which it is subject really touch the root of the matter. I hope to show that, in spite of all that is human about it, there is more that is Divine. The body, the outward form, may be of the earth earthy, but the spirit by which it is pervaded and animated is from heaven. This too, believe me, is no mere matter of assumption or speculation. It is proved in the same way as that by which we prove the presence of a human element. And if I fail in conveying that proof in all its cogency, the fault will be mine.

NOTE.

THE gradual nature of the steps which lead up from questions of what is called the Lower Criticism (which deals with the *text*) to questions of the Higher Criticism (which deals with *authorship*, &c.), and the difficulty of drawing a hard and fast line between them will be understood from the following examples.

(a) I St. John v. 7.   The three Heavenly Witnesses (*comma Johanneum*).

Now almost universally given up on grounds of External Evidence (immense preponderance of testimony against the words which are only found in

two Greek MSS., one of the fifteenth and one of the
sixteenth century, though going back as far as the
fourth century in Latin) + Internal Evidence (break
in the continuity of the passage).

The words were originally a gloss, or comment, suggested by the text and written in the margin, but
afterwards mistaken for part of the text and inserted
with it.

(β) St. John vii. 53—viii. 11. The section of the Woman
taken in Adultery (*pericope adulterae*).

Rejected by nearly all critical authorities on the
ground of

External Evidence (all Greek MSS. older than the
eighth century, except one which has Latin affinities,
and many express statements) + Internal Evidence
(inappropriate break in the context).

Originally a narrative derived fiom some other early
source, transcribed in the margin to illustrate the
saying, *I judge no man* (St. John viii. 15); thence
transferred to the text at the nearest place where an
insertion could be made.

(γ) St. Mark xvi. 9–20. The Last Twelve Verses of St.
Mark.

Rejected by many critical authorities on the ground
of

External Evidence (absence not from many MSS., but
from the two best, some express patristic statements,
and the presence of an alternative ending to the
Gospel in a few MSS.) + Internal Evidence (especially the abrupt beginning, which has been anticipated in ver. 1).

If the verses are not genuine, we must suppose that

the original ending to the Gospel had been torn away or become illegible, and that they were added to supply its place.

(δ) Romans xv, xvi. and especially xvi. 1–16 (or 3–16). Supposed by some critics not to have been originally part of the Epistle to the Romans on the ground of

Slight External Evidence (the position of the closing doxology, xvi. 25–27, in a few MSS. at the end of ch. xiv. or at both places) + Internal Evidence (the difficulty of accounting for the number of greetings which St. Paul is sending to a Church which he had not yet visited).

Several explanations are proposed for the section as it stands if not original : some believe it to belong to a letter written at a later date to Rome ; others believe it to be part of a letter addressed by St. Paul to Ephesus.

(ε) 2 Corinthians vi. 14—vii. 1. Supposed by two or three critics not to belong to this Epistle on the ground of

Purely Internal Evidence (break in the continuity of the argument).

Some of those who hold this view believe the verses to be a fragment of the lost letter alluded to in 1 Cor. v. 9, with which they would agree in subject. A discussion of this theory has been recently carried on in the pages of the *Classical Review.*

(ζ) 1 Samuel xvii. 1—xviii. 5. Large portions of this passage are omitted in the best MS. of the Septuagint, Cod. Vaticanus (B.), and there are some marks of omission in other MSS.

It is probable, on the whole, that the verses are

genuine, and that they were omitted in some very early Greek or Hebrew MSS. in order to escape a difficulty in harmonizing the contents of this section with 1 Sam. xvi. 14–23.

(η) Passages like this last lead us up to questions such as that as to the authorship of Isa. xl–lxvi. or Zech. ix–xiv, which turn entirely upon Internal Evidence (difference of style and difference in the historical situation from the rest of the book).

As soon as books began to be written in vellum volumes, or *codices*, shaped like our present books, it is easy enough to understand how writings came to be attributed to wrong authors. These books were of considerable size, and would hold several treatises. Three or four by some well-known author would be written first: then would come an anony-mous treatise: the original scribe would know it to be anonymous, but the next-comer would suppose it to be by the author whose name stood at the head of the volume, and would quote it as such. This would hold good from the fourth century onwards. The process would not be quite so easy in the earlier period, when the usual form for books was that of the roll, which was smaller in size. Still, the same sort of thing no doubt took place. Two writings would be supposed to have the same author, simply because they lay side by side in the same case or were otherwise brought into juxtaposition. It was a mistake, but an accidental mistake, and involves no suspicion of bad faith.

III.

THE DIVINE ELEMENT GENERALLY CONSIDERED.

(Whitehall, August 3, 1890.)

2 CORINTHIANS iv. 7, R. V.

We have this treasure in earthen vessels, that the exceeding greatness of the power may be of God, and not from ourselves.

THE fundamental mistake that is too often made is to form the idea of what Inspiration is from what we should antecedently expect it to be and not from the evidence to what as a matter of fact it is. It is hardly a century and a half since Bishop Butler showed in his masterly way the precariousness of arguments of this kind. We are not competent judges before the fact of the method of God's dealings with men. In the world of nature there are a thousand things which are different from what we should have expected. We see but a little corner, but an infinitesimal part of the universal frame of things. We know not what lies behind and beyond. There are doubtless hidden harmonies of which we have no cognisance, far-off goals which lie beyond our ken. If we had but fuller glimpses into these,

many of the perplexities which now surround us
might well be explained. If we believe in God, as
we needs must believe in Him, there are many of
His ways which we must simply take upon trust,
confident that all things really *work together for
good*, however much we see or fail to see by what
processes the end is attained. The point is soon
reached where we can only bow our heads in silent
acceptance of the Divine Will.

But if this is true of the works of God it holds
good equally of His word. History is strewn with
warnings as to the mistakes in which we are involved
the moment we begin to lay down what an Inspired
Book ought to be and what it ought not to be. I
spoke of some of these mistakes last time. They
are all so many applications of the assumption that
an Inspired Book must be infallible, not merely as a
Revelation but as a Book. Is there any better
reason for this than there was for those other assumptions which Bishop Butler showed to be so untenable
—that a revelation from God must be universal, that
it could not be confined to an obscure and insigni-
ficant people ; that a revelation from God must be
clear—that it could not be wrapt up in difficulties of
interpretation ; that its evidence must be certain
and such as should leave no room for doubt [1] ? All
these criteria had been actually put forward ; the

[1] See especially *Analogy of Religion*, Part II. Chap. iii.

Christian revelation had been tried by them and
found wanting.   No one would think of putting
forward any such criteria now.   Yet there is no
essential difference between the claim which was
then made for the Revelation itself, and the claim
which is still made for the Book in which that Revelation is embodied.   Such a Book, it is urged, must
at the least be infallible.   If that were so, we should
find it hard to contend with the facts ; for the sphere
of its infallibility has been steadily narrowed.   Its
text is not infallible ; its grammar is not infallible ; its
science is not infallible ; and there is grave question
whether its history is altogether infallible.   But to
argue thus is to take up a false position from the
outset.   It is far better not to ask at all what an Inspired Book ought to be, but to content ourselves with
the enquiry what this Book, which comes to us as inspired, in fact and reality is.   It will not refuse to
answer our questions.

Let us look at the matter in the first instance broadly,
and then examine it in somewhat closer detail[1].

When the first Christians went about with their
little cases packed with rolls, some more and some
fewer, and when they placed these precious writings

---

[1] An argument similar to that which follows will be found, stated
with great force and ability, in the early lectures of a volume, which has
appeared since this was written, by Dr. R. W. Dale, *The Living Christ
and the Four Gospels* (London, 1890).

in the hands of the pagans with whom they came in contact, and begged them to read and study them, what sort of impression do we suppose that the reading made upon a candid mind? When our own missionaries distribute Bibles and Testaments, and those to whom they are given take them into some quiet corner and scrutinize their pages, what is it for which they look and what is it that they find? Or without letting our imagination travel so far, without going beyond our own English homes, there is one volume which occupies an honoured place in them, which lies beside the sick-bed or the armchair, and ministers solace to the aged and suffering, or instruction to the young. If we were to ask any of these what it was that came home to them in the Bible, we should not find them troubling their heads as to details of chronology or archaeology, we should not find them speculating as to the exact wording of a text or as to the process by which some of the Books had assumed their present form, neither should we find them attacking the question in strictly logical order and beginning with the enquiry what ground there was for the authority which the Bible claimed; but they would tell us that there was a great deal perhaps which they could not understand, but yet that there were sayings on every page, not few or far between, but constantly occurring, which spoke to their hearts with power.

Now of course it is true that every one who is given
to reading books at all knows of many which have
exercised a very considerable effect upon him. There
are collections of 'wit and wisdom' to which he may
turn if he will—or he will have his own collections
stored away in the chambers of his brain. There
will be included among these a number of sayings
which at one time or another, as Sir Philip Sidney
said, have stirred his blood 'as with the sound of a
trumpet.' The Bible contains a vast number of such
sayings, full of ripe insight and wisdom, such as this :
*The heart knoweth its own bitterness, and a stranger
doth not intermeddle with its joy*[1]*;* or this : *It is better
to go to the house of mourning than to go to the house
of feasting . . . Sorrow is better than laughter : for by
the sadness of the countenance the heart is made
better*[2].

Sayings like this are thickly scattered over books,
for instance, like Proverbs, which do not hold at all
the highest place in the volume. And then again in
the histories there are narratives full of chivalrous
courage like the meeting of David and Goliath, or
wonderfully tender and touching, like the discovery
of Joseph to his brethren, the parting of Ruth and
Naomi, the friendship of David and Jonathan.

It may be doubted whether on this level of common
human interest there is any other book which on the

[1] Prov. xiv. 10.   [2] Eccl. vii. 2–3.

whole is so rich as the Bible. But if that were all
it still would not have a unique place among books.
The Bible and Shakespeare might be on the same
footing as part of an Englishman's library.

But then there is another class of sayings different
in kind from these, and with no such direct parallels.
*Blessed is he whose unrighteousness is forgiven and
whose sin is covered. Blessed is the man unto whom
the Lord imputeth no sin*[1]. *Like as a father pitieth
his children, so the Lord pitieth them that fear Him*[2].
*The Son of Man is come to seek and to save that
which was lost*[3]. *And He said to me, My grace is
sufficient for thee, for My strength is made perfect in
weakness*[4].

These are thoughts that move in a new region.
They are something more than the formulated teaching of experience, 'the harvest of a quiet eye' brood-
ing over the lessons which life has brought. They
tell of an experience indeed, but experience of a
different kind—an experience not easily reached, nay,
such as could not be reached at all except by ways
of which the world knows nothing. The sense of
forgiveness, the consciousness of Divine Love, the
assurance that there *is* a deliverance for the lost and
erring, self-surrender to a Power *outside* self which
supplements and supports the infirmities of human

---

[1] Ps. xxxii. 1, 2.   [2] Ps. ciii. 13.
[3] St. Luke xix. 10.   [4] 2 Cor. xii. 9.

nature—not only are these experiences which belong
not to the ordinary every-day intercourse of men
with men, but to the higher Life of the Spirit : more
than this, they imply a system of things, a series of
Divine interpositions, in which man is passive and not
active, a recipient rather than an originator. We are
reminded of the teaching of St. John's Gospel : *He
came unto His own (land) and His own (people) received Him not. But as many as received Him to them
gave He the right to become children of God, even to
those that believe on His Name ; which were born not
of blood, nor of the will of the flesh, nor of the will of
man, but of God*[1]. And again of the High-Priestly
prayer : *O righteous Father, the world knew Thee not,
but I knew Thee : and these know that Thou didst send
Me*[2].

There are two spheres. There is the sphere of
what St. John calls *the world*, and what St. Paul
calls the *natural man*, the sphere of eating and drink-
ing, of marrying and giving in marriage, the sphere
of trade, of pleasure, of science, of politics ; and there
is the other sphere intersecting this, though distinct
from it, the sphere of a higher, finer spiritual life in
which *they sow not, neither do they spin.*

The Bible, every one who reads it must feel, is
charged with affirmations about this supersensual
sphere. Those affirmations do not hang in the air.

[1] St. John i. 11–13.   [2] St. John xvii. 25.

They are not merely such 'stuff as dreams are made of.' They rest upon a foundation of fact.

The facts in question are not isolated or disconnected. They form a chain, a continuous history stretching back far into the past, culminating in the events of a few short years of which there has come down to us what we have reason to believe is a veracious record ; again, descending from that culmination downwards, still in continuous sequence, to our own day and generation. We have this guarantee that, though spiritual, though ideal, the phenomena of which we speak are not unreal. They could not have played the part they have in the lives of so many millions of men and women if they were. They rest on facts— the facts of the divinely-ordered history of a divinely-chosen nation ; the facts of the Life and Death of Christ, and of the founding and subsequent history of the Christian Church : they run into facts, facts of living experience, such as, for all their delicacy, the eye may see and the ear may hear.

Here is a fabric standing over against the other, a 'new creation' within the old. In a book like Shakespeare's Plays we have the interpretation of the one : in the Bible we have the interpretation of the other. This it is which has made the Bible so precious to the thousands and tens of thousands who have used it. The question of interest to them has not been what sort of external attestation it brought with it,

but what was its inner verisimilitude. As an interpretation of the spiritual life, was it true, was it
adequate? Again we appeal to the testimony of
the millions of men and women living or who once
lived, who have found it both true and adequate. It
has been at least to them,

> 'The fountain-light of all their day,
> The master-light of all their seeing.'

Science may demand something more: it may demand
credentials formally proved ; it may demand investigations rigorously conducted; it may have its questions of
canonicity and authenticity; it may insist on compari-
sons with other sacred books and other religions. The
demand is a legitimate one, and must not be rejected
or ignored. It is to be hoped that our Christian
Faith will always have its philosophy for the
philosophers, its logic for the logicians, its learning
for the learned. But plain men and women will take
their own short cut for determining whether or no
the Bible is divine. Does it prove itself to be divine
to me? Has it proved itself to be divine to others
like me? The answer to this half at least of the
challenge cannot be uncertain. Already in the
Apostolic age there was a writer who appealed to a
cloud of witnesses. How many generations have
passed since then, and how has that cloud of witnesses spread and expanded! Comparing what it
is now with what it was then is like comparing the

speck no bigger than a man's hand with the whole sky overcast and the sound of abundance of rain.

Strictly speaking, in the logical order of things, in that order which we are apt to assume but which as a matter of fact few really follow, all this would come in better as a confirmation or verification of truths otherwise arrived at. In the present course it might from some points of view come in more appropriately after rather than before what I hope to say next Sunday. It is an argument which at first sight appears popular rather than scientific. And yet it has, I cannot but think, a justification in philosophy as well as in practice. Truth, when we come to think of it, is really nothing more than propositions framed in accordance with the ascertained laws of the human mind. The inner truth of things in themselves we cannot know, or at least can only infer remotely. What we are concerned with primarily, if not entirely, is the impressions made upon our own minds. But, if that is so, surely the experimental test is of the very greatest importance, especially where the question is of a theory which is to cover the *whole of life.* It is natural to ask in regard to such a theory.before anything else, Does it *work?* Does it really harmonize with the conditions of human nature? Does it really result in a type of life and character which gives satisfaction to those who attain to it and commands the respect of those

who do not? If this mode of arguing appears unphilo-
sophical the fault is really in the philosophies, which
isolate a very small part of human nature and treat it
as if it could lay down laws for the whole. The
reason why people cling to old beliefs, as it sometimes
seems irrationally, is because in mental processes
of this kind there is much that enters in unconsciously besides the elements of which we are
conscious. A sound philosophy ought to widen itself
out so as to give some account of this. But when
that comes to be done with Christianity, and with the
Bible as the foundation of Christianity, all this
experimental testing supplied by the lives of so many
myriads of human beings is an enormous weight in
the scale. If it is instinct—even as we say a 'blind,'
that is, an 'unconscious' instinct which makes it
possess such an attraction for them, that instinct must
have its causes and cannot rest on mere delusion.

The questions which at present are agitating
men's minds only touch the fringe of this immense
mass of testimony. They are really questions of
detail. They may mean perhaps a little more
here, a little less there. They do, I admit, take
away something of the definiteness and certainty
with which men were wont to appeal to their Bibles;
but I shall endeavour to show that there are com-
pensations for the loss. Definiteness is not always
a gain : the certainty which springs from the absence

of questioning and of search is a different thing from
the certainty which comes after search and enquiry.
And the latter kind of certainty is, we may be sure,
the higher and better of the two.

I will make bold to use a comparison, which, if it
is rightly applied, will leave no doubt on which side
the advantage lies. When our Lord condescended
to become Incarnate upon earth, He found the Jews
in the possession of an elaborate code of law by
which they were in the habit of directing their lives.
When they wished to know what to do in any case
they turned its pages till they found a precept corresponding to that case. His coming was the end
of the Law ; it abolished all that code and did away
with the precepts on which the Scribes and Pharisees
had been wont to lean. And yet, in the very act of
abolishing the Law, Jesus said, *I am not come to destroy
but to fulfil.* How so ? He fulfilled the Law, while
He abolished it, by substituting *principles for precepts.*
He fulfilled it when He said, *Thou shalt love the Lord
thy God with all thy heart and thy neighbour as
thyself,* and when He set in motion forces which gave
men the *capacity* for loving God and their neighbour.

Now it seems to me that if what the critics say
is true, the change in the use of the Bible will be
only of the same kind. It will substitute principles
for precepts. It will no longer be so easy to find
proof-texts for this or that ; but the principles which

run through the Bible will be better understood
and more vigorously realized ; they will be held with
a stronger and a firmer faith. The mechanical and
verbal inspiration of the Bible may be questioned,
but its real and. vital inspiration will shine out as
it has never done [1].

[1] No doubt there is a relative justification, similar in kind to that
which has just been urged in this lecture for other religions besides
Christianity.   Mahometanism we need not count, because its best
elements are common to Christianity and derived either from it or from
Judaism.   But Buddhism may allege with good reason the number of
its votaries.   It is impossible to read the life and teaching of Gautama
without feeling that he too had an impulse from the Holy One.   It
would be little in accordance with Christian doctrine to maintain that
the divine influences which were vouchsafed in so large a measure to
select spirits in Palestine were wholly wanting in India or Greece.

But the highest of faiths must be tested by the hold which they take
on the most widely cultured nations.   Christianity succeeded to the
spiritual inheritance of Greece and Rome ; and the experiments which
have been made, not only by Christian missionaries, but by native move-
ments like the Brahmo Somaj, all go to encourage the hope that it is
capable of succeeding, and will one day succeed, to the spiritual inheritance of the Oriental peoples.   For a fuller discussion of the relation
of Biblical Inspiration to the phenomena which resemble it in non-
Christian religions, see Lecture VII.

IV.

THE DIVINE ELEMENT IN ITS SPECIAL
MANIFESTATIONS.

(Whitehall, August 3, 1890.)

2 St. Peter i. 21.

No prophecy ever came by the will of man, but men spake from God, being moved by the Holy Ghost.

IF what has been hitherto urged is true, we may lay it down as a fundamental principle that a true conception of what the Bible is must be obtained from the Bible itself. There is no reason to be afraid of going straight to the Bible; and there is, I think, no reason to be afraid of putting to it a direct question, even though it may involve something that might be called 'criticism.' Provided that we go to it with complete singleness of purpose, with a perfectly clear and open mind, not seeking merely to establish a case either on the one side or on the other, but simply to learn the truth, we shall be guilty of no irreverence, and it would be a want of faith to say that we were endangering anything sacred. Truth is not such a brittle thing that it must break in pieces as

soon as it begins to be handled. Nor can we think
that He who has given to us the Bible will have left
His own image and superscription upon it so faint
that the observant eye cannot see it.

Certainly He has not done this. A more welcome
duty awaits me now than that in which I have been
engaged hitherto. I may now put the question,
What proof have we that the Bible is really the Word
of God, and that His voice has really spoken to us
in its pages? It seems to me that the clearest and
simplest and most direct proof—apart from the verification supplied to it by history—is to be found in
the account which the sacred writers give us of themselves. The central phenomenon of the Old Testament is Prophecy. And the prophets have left us
very clear statements of the relation in which they
stood to the Almighty Power whose will they claimed
to interpret. The leading Prophets all tell us under
what circumstances they came to assume their office,
and how they came to regard themselves as exponents of the Divine Will. The first on the line is
Moses, that typical figure on which—as you will
remember from Deut. xviii. 18—not only the whole
succeeding revelation of the Old Testament, but even
the culmination of Prophecy in the New Testament,
was to be modelled. The Call of Moses is a familiar
story. He was feeding his flock on the scanty
herbage found here and there among the mountains

in the heart of the Sinaitic peninsula when a remarkable sight arrested his attention. The organ of
vision may have been the eye of the spirit and not
the bodily eye. To the men whose writing has come
down to us the Bible, the things of the spirit, were
so near and so intensely realized, and their way of
expressing themselves is so simple—suited to the
primitive age in which they lived and to which their
message was addressed—that they were not careful
to distinguish between the two as we, with our more
precise definition of the human faculties, should be
bound to do. An awful voice—again as we may
well think heard by the spirit and not by any bodily
sense—comes to him and delivers to him at once a
revelation and a commission [1]. To appreciate the
full depth of the revelation would require a long enquiry into which I cannot now stay to enter. It was the
custom in those early days to compress any weighty
truth as to the being and attributes of God into a
Name. And so the delivery of this Name I AM
THAT I AM marked an epoch in the history of Israel,
a new step in the process by which divine things
were disclosed to them. But the point which I desire more especially to notice is the reluctance of
Moses to accept the commission that is offered to
him. *And Moses said unto God, Who am I that I
should go unto Pharaoh, and that I should bring forth*

[1] On this see Driver in *Studia Biblica*, I. p. 1, esp. pp. 17-18.

E

the children of Israel out of Egypt[1]*?* And then
follows a long expostulation in which one difficulty
after another is raised. Moses ends by pleading his
incapacity of speech. *Oh Lord, I am not eloquent,
neither heretofore, nor since Thou hast spoken unto Thy
servant: for I am slow of speech and of a slow tongue.
And the Lord said unto him, Who hath made man's
mouth? or who maketh a man dumb or deaf or seeing
or blind? is it not I the Lord? Now therefore go and
I will be with thy mouth and teach thee what thou
shalt speak.* A last desperate effort to evade the
responsibility—*And he said, Oh Lord, send, I pray
Thee, by the hand of him whom Thou wilt send.* And
we read that *the anger of the Lord was kindled against
Moses, and He said, Is there not Aaron thy brother,
the Levite? . . . He shall be thy spokesman unto the
people*[2].

The impression conveyed by the narrative clearly
is that the whole *rôle* of a prophet is *forced* upon
Moses very much against his will. It precludes, as
strongly as anything could preclude, the supposition
that the weighty message which Moses delivered to
his contemporaries and the revolution which he
wrought by it was purely a product of his own
imagination. Nothing can be clearer than that the
opposite of this was the case. Moses was really an
instrument in the hand of God, and the words which

---

[1] Exodus iii. 11.   [2] Exodus iv. 10–16.

were put in his mouth to speak were put there by the Divine Spirit.

It might be said perhaps, if any one were disposed to play the part of an objector, that, according to the newer views of criticism, the narrative was not set down in writing by Moses himself, but only after a considerable interval of time, and that we have no guarantee that it is an exact representation of the facts. However this may be, I think we shall admit that there is a remarkable verisimilitude about it, that it corresponds in a striking manner to the analogies of other great religious crises of the kind, and that whatever intermediate steps may separate the narrative, as we have it, from Moses himself, it must be taken as a history which is in essence and substance true, and that it does not err in ascribing the origin of the movement of which Moses was the visible human centre to direct Divine intervention[1].

The next witness to which I shall appeal is not open to any such exception. There is no doubt that the 6th chapter of Isaiah was actually written by the prophet, and it describes his call just as the narrative in the Book of Exodus describes the call of Moses. The two narratives are so wholly different in the range of their symbolism and in their outward setting that no one would think of suggesting the literary dependence of the one upon the other ; and yet when

---

[1] See the authorities quoted by Fisher, *Nature*, &c. p. 25 f.

they come to be examined the fundamental lines of the two passages, the nature of the relation between the prophet and the source of his inspiration, are the same. It is made equally clear that the inspiration comes from without and not from within. The prophet himself is equally reluctant; he is equally conscious of inability and unworthiness; but this consciousness of his is overcome by what we are obliged to regard as supernatural means. When he is prostrate before the vision of the Divine Glory he cries out, *Woe is me! for I am undone; because I am a man of unclean lips, and I dwell in the midst of a people of unclean lips: for mine eyes have seen the King, the Lord of Hosts.* But in the midst of this self-abasement he sees a seraph, as it were, flying towards him with a live coal from off the altar. With this his lips are touched, and he is told that his iniquity is taken away and his sin purged. Then he receives his message.

It is extraordinary how, one after another, the same features are reproduced in the prophetic books. The process is always extremely different from what it would be if the prophet arrived at his insight into spiritual things by the tentative efforts of his own genius. There is something sharp and sudden about it. He can lay his finger, so to speak, upon the moment when it came. And it always comes in the form of an overpowering force from without, against which he struggles but in vain. Listen to this, for instance, from the opening of the Book of Jeremiah : *Now the word of the Lord came unto me, saying, Before I formed thee in the belly I knew thee, and before thou camest forth out of the womb I sanctified thee : I have appointed thee a prophet unto the nations. Then said I, Ah, Lord God! behold I cannot speak: for I am a child. But the Lord said unto me, Say not, I am a child: for to whomsoever I shall send thee thou shalt go, and whatsoever I shall command thee thou shalt speak.* The tender, humble spirit of Jeremiah deprecates the high commission which is being pressed upon him, but he cannot refuse it. He must needs testify at the peril of his life before kings and princes and people. But the words put in his mouth are not his own. *Behold, I have put My words in thy mouth: see, I have this day set thee over the nations and over the kingdoms, to pluck up and to break down, and to destroy and to overthrow; to build and to plant*[1].

Read through in like manner the first two chapters of the prophecy of Ezekiel. Here perhaps the main idea is suggested by Isaiah, though an individual stamp is put upon it. The dating is even more precise ; it was in the fifth day of the fourth month of the fifth year of Jehoiachim's captivity that the great vision with which his book opens was vouchsafed to

[1] Jeremiah i. 5-10.

the prophet and the roll given to him which contained his message.

It is not, however, only at the beginning of his
career that the prophet passes through a crisis which
is clearly not self-caused. Scattered all through the
prophetic writings are expressions which speak of
some strong and irresistible impulse coming down
upon the prophet, determining his attitude to the
events of his time, constraining his utterance, making
his words the vehicle of a higher meaning than their
own. For instance this of Isaiah's: *The Lord spake
thus to me with a strong hand*—an emphatic phrase
which denotes the over-mastering nature of the impulse—*The Lord spake thus to me with a strong hand,
and instructed me that I should·not walk in the way
of this people* [1]. Or, again, take this of Jeremiah's:
*I sat not in the assembly of them that make merry
nor rejoiced; I sat alone because of Thy hand; for
Thou hast filled me with indignation* [2]. Or passages
like these from Ezekiel: *So the Spirit lifted me up,
and took me away; and I went in bitterness, in the
heat of my spirit, and the hand of the Lord was
strong upon me* [3]. *And it came to pass*—on a given
day—*as I sat in mine house, and the elders of Judah
sat before me, that the hand of the Lord God fell there
upon me* [4]. The one standing characteristic of the

[1] Isaiah viii. 11.   [2] Jeremiah xv. 17.
[3] Ezekiel iii. 14.   [4] Ezekiel viii. 1. (Riehm, p. 211.)

prophet is that he speaks with the authority of Jehovah Himself. This is part of the promise made to Moses : *I will raise them up a prophet from among their brethren, like unto thee; and I will put My words in his mouth, and he shall speak unto them all that I shall command him. And it shall come to pass, that whosoever will not hearken to My words which he shall speak in My name, I will require it of him. But the prophet which shall speak a word pre-sumptuously in My name, which I have not com-manded him to speak, or that shall speak in the name of other gods, that same prophet shall die* [1]. Hence it is that the prophets one and all preface their addresses so confidently, *The Word of the Lord,* or *Thus saith the Lord.* They have even the au-dacity to speak in the first person, as if Jehovah Himself were speaking. As in Isaiah, *Hearken unto Me, O Jacob, and Israel my called; I am He, I am the first, I also am the last* [2], and so on. The per-sonality of the prophet sinks entirely into the back-ground ; he feels himself for the time being the mouthpiece of the Almighty. Imagine any one doing this in the present day. When we quote the Bible indeed we may say *Thus saith the Lord.* But if any one presumed to use such language, not quoting the Bible, we should say that he was either an impostor or mad. The prophets were certainly not impostors,

---

[1] Deut. xviii. 18–20.   [2] Isaiah xlviii. 12

and they were certainly not mad. They were not impostors, because their words often brought them only mockery, abuse, imprisonment, and even death. And they were not mad. Nothing could be more simple or more sincere—more sane we might say— than the language which they use; there is not the slightest trace of a morbid consciousness about it. The effort, so far as there is an effort, is not to *claim* a revelation but to escape it. And we, looking back at this distance of time, can see more clearly than it was possible for their contemporaries to see that they spoke the words of truth and soberness. Words more sublime or more really illuminative never fell from the lips of man.

I have taken the prophets as the typical example of Old Testament religion, because in them we can see the process that we call 'Inspiration' most distinctly; but the imperatives of the Law, *Thou shalt*, and *Thou shalt not*, are essentially of the same kind. Of the same kind it is too, for instance, in the Book of Proverbs when Wisdom is introduced as speaking: *Doth not wisdom cry, and understanding put forth her voice? In the top of high places by the way, where the paths meet she standeth . . . Unto you, O men, I call; and thy voice is to the sons of men*[1]. And yet more distinctly does the spirit of prophecy breathe in the Psalter, for it is a Psalm of David (recorded in

[1] Proverbs viii. 1, 2, 4.

2 Sam. xxiii) which begins, *The Spirit of the Lord spake by me, and His word was upon my tongue.* Compare again this from the Book of Job describing one of the more agitating modes of revelation: *Now a thing was secretly brought to me and mine ear received a whisper thereof. In thoughts from the vision of the night, when deep sleep falleth on men, fear came upon me, and trembling, which made all my bones to shake. Then a spirit* (or *a breath*) *passed before my face; the hair of my flesh stood up. It stood still, but I could not discern the appearance thereof: a form was before mine eyes; I heard a still voice saying, Shall a mortal man be more just than God? Shall a man be more pure than his Maker*[1]*?* It is true that this is an imaginative description, and that it is put in the mouth of Eliphaz and not of Job, but it shows how deeply rooted was the conviction that all prophetic revelations had an external source, and the exalted teaching which follows is well worthy of such an origin. The prophecies of Balaam are another striking testimony to the same conviction.

We are apt to think of the New Testament as if it were different from the Old. We think of it too as authoritative; but we invest it with a different kind of authority. We forget, however, that the Spirit of Prophecy was just as active in the New Testament times as under the older dispensation. The pheno-

[1] Job iv. 12-17.

mena may have been a little more varied, but the
source of the phenomena was the same. The apostles
themselves regarded the out-pouring of the Spirit,
of which they themselves were partakers, as a direct
fulfilment of the prophecy of Joel, *I will pour forth
of My Spirit upon all flesh: and your sons and your
daughters shall prophesy, and your young men shall
see visions, and your old men shall dream dreams:
Yea, and on My servants and on My handmaidens
in those days will I pour forth of My Spirit; and they
shall prophesy* [1]. It would be easy to show by
detailed examples how God made known His will
by precisely the same methods as those which were
in use among the Old Testament prophets; by symbolical acts, as in the case of Agabus binding himself
with St. Paul's girdle, in visions as to St. Peter and
repeatedly to St. Paul, by sudden irresistible impulse,
as in the case of the girl with the spirit of divination,
sometimes even by the mouth of unconscious and
hostile witnesses, as in the memorable words of
Caiaphas, who spoke not knowing what he said.
And not only so, but the main drift of New Testament revelation was really an expression of prophecy.
The testimony of Jesus is the Spirit of prophecy, said
the seer of the Apocalypse [2]. We know that St. Paul
was richly endowed with this gift, and when we look
into his Epistles we see that they were really pro-

---

[1] Acts ii. 17, 18.   [2] Rev. xix. 10.

phetic writings just as much as the works of the elder prophets. Let us read his own account of his own call, and compare it, for instance, with that of Jeremiah. We have it in the first chapter of the Epistle to the Galatians : *I make known to you, brethren, as touching the gospel which was preached by me, that it is not after man. For neither did I receive it from man, nor was I taught it, but it came to me through revelation of Jesus Christ. For ye have heard of my manner of life in time past in the Jews' religion, how that beyond measure I persecuted the Church of God . . . but when it was the good pleasure of God, Who separated me from my mother's womb, and called me through His grace*—you will remember Jeremiah's *Before I formed thee in the belly I knew thee, and before thou camest forth from the womb I sanctified thee—when it pleased God to reveal His Son in me that I might preach Him among the Gentiles; immediately I conferred not with flesh and blood*[1], and so on. Clearly the revelation, or series of revelations, by which there was brought home to the mind of St. Paul the full significance of his Master's mission, was the same in kind as that of the I AM THAT I AM of Moses, or the WONDERFUL, COUNSELLOR of Isaiah. It was not merely a product of his own brain. Of him too it might be said, as it was said to St. Peter after his confession, *Flesh and*

[1] Gal. i. 11-13, 15, 16.

blood hath not revealed it unto thee, but My Father Which is in Heaven[1].

When we think of it, this continuity of the Bible from first to last is exceedingly impressive. It forces in upon the mind a conviction, which cannot easily be shaken, that there has been at work in it something 'more than natural,' the influence — the sustained and vitalizing influence—of a Higher Power. I said a moment ago that the prophets of the Old Testament were not impostors and were not mad. We may say the same of the writers of the New Testament. They too were not drunk with new wine, but the wine with which they were really filled and intoxicated was the wine of the Spirit. They assure us that they spoke *as the Spirit gave them utterance.* And all that we do is to take them at their word. When we say that they were 'moved by the Holy Ghost,' we mean by it what they meant, neither less nor more.

[1] Matt. xvi. 17.

V.

THE BLENDING OF HUMAN AND DIVINE.

(Whitehall, August 10, 1890.)

2 PETER i. 19, R. V.

*And we have the word of prophecy made more sure; where-
unto ye do well that ye take heed, as unto a lamp shining in a
dark place.*

MY purpose so far, and especially in the last of
these discourses, has been to speak a word of re-
assurance to those who look with concern at the
direction which Biblical enquiry is taking. The idea
is too prevalent that if once free criticism is admitted
a process is begun which will end in the destruction
of all religious belief whatsoever. The process is apt
to look too much like an inclined plane, of which we
see the top but do not see the bottom. There are
many anxious minds who fear that when once belief
begins to slide it will find itself before it knows
precipitated into the abyss. This is the apprehension
which I have tried to show to be unfounded ; I have
tried to show that we *do* see what lies at the bottom
of the incline, that there is a point where Criticism of

its own accord must come to a standstill. That point I found last time in the consciousness of the sacred writers themselves. It seems to me that this is the true starting-point for a really critical enquiry into the nature of Biblical inspiration. The advantage of it is that it assumes nothing. It takes the documents just as they stand. It is quite willing to make any necessary allowance for dates and manner of composition. But practically, as we saw, these literary considerations make no difference. The great bulk of the evidence is unimpeachable on this score, and its tenor is too clear to be mistaken. The Biblical writers themselves were convinced that the words which they spoke were put into their mouths by God. They speak in accents of perfect confidence and perfect sincerity. There is none of the straining of personal assumption about them. They take no credit for it. In the most conspicuous instances there is not only no eagerness to claim inspiration, but a positive shrinking from it. This reluctance is in each case overborne by a Power which the writer feels to be outside himself. The Spirit of the Lord took hold of them and made them for the time being its organs. This was their own belief. And looking back upon their words in the light thrown upon them by history we cannot think that they were wrong.

Here it seems to me that we have a clear standing ground. There is no need to have recourse to any doubtful theories of external authority. We appeal to the Bible ; and the Bible bears witness, and satisfactory witness, to itself.

But having gone so far as this our attention must now be turned to another side of the problem. If we come back to the Bible again, and again interrogate it to see what answer it makes to our enquiries, shall we find that room is left for the phenomena which recent criticism believes itself to have discovered in it? Is there anything which the Bible lays down in point of doctrine which would conflict with these phenomena in point of fact? In other words, do they imply an extension of the human element in Scripture inconsistent with that Divine element which asserts its presence so unmistakeably?

I have said that the typical expression of this Divine element in the Bible is Prophecy. Other forms of Biblical literature partake of it by virtue of their share in the prophetic spirit. Now prophecy certainly has its own limitations. The gift of prophecy was a special gift in reference to particular circumstances. It was called forth by those circumstances ; and if it looked beyond them it did so as giving expression to principles which were capable of a wider application than the particular issue ; but it was very far from implying universal knowledge. The fundamental point in the activity of the Prophet was his insight into the principles which lay behind the

Divine ordering of events. His knowledge of these principles was borne in upon his mind in a way that he felt to be due to an influence from without. He knew that all that he said in reference to them was put into his mouth by God. There was also perhaps something more than this. The prophet was in part the conscious organ of the Divine Will; and it would seem that he was also in part an unconscious organ of the same Will. If he was gifted with a peculiar insight into the workings of God's Providence, so also is it open to us to believe that he was himself included in the sphere of those workings, so that utterances which from his point of view and from the point of view of the immediate circumstances might have been described as accidental were not really accidental but bore relation to some more distant part of the Divine plan. I mean that, for instance, when the Psalmist says, *They pierced my hands and my feet,* or *They parted my garments among them,* he may not have been himself thinking of the Death of the Messiah, and yet his words and the facts corresponding to them may have been overruled so as to be rightly applied to features in the Death of the Messiah [1]. But to say this is a very different thing from saying that a prophet possessed 'all mysteries and all knowledge' besides those of

[1] See especially Essay iii. on 'The Christian Element in the Book of Isaiah' in Cheyne's *Isaiah,* vol. ii.

which the Spirit of God made him the special vehicle. He spoke the words that were put into his mouth, but outside those words and outside the range of facts which came under the same general principles as those to which he was giving utterance, his knowledge did not differ from that possessed by the rest of his contemporaries. We must dismiss from our minds the idea that the prophet possessed a knowledge of all truth, even of all religious truth, much less of all truth unconnected with religion. He was the organ of a particular revelation which God vouchsafed to make at a particular place and time, but it is only the *sum* of such revelations that makes up the whole body of religious truth as we have it in the Bible. It was not given all at once, but at *sundry times and in divers manners.*

Only One there was to Whom the Spirit of God was given without measure. Only One there was upon Whom the spiritual eye might have seen the angels ascending and descending and keeping up a constant communication with the Father all through His earthly career. What Jacob saw in a certain memorable vision at a turning-point in his life, that was given to the Prophet of Nazareth all through. But in this He was unique, and we must not argue from Him even to the greatest of His servants. The very frequency of that expression, *The word of the Lord came* to this or that among the prophets shows

F

what wide spaces of time there must have been when
no word came, when there was *neither voice, nor any
to answer, nor any that regarded.* Jeremiah tells us
that on one occasion when he was consulted upon a
point directly connected with the main subject of his
mission, he had to wait ten days before any revelation
came to him [1].

There are some significant places in the New
Testament from which a light is reflected back upon
the Old.   For instance in the Epistle to the Romans,
where St. Paul bids his converts *prophesy according to
the measure of [their] faith;* or again where he speaks
of himself and the Apostles as preaching *each as the
Lord gave to him* [2]*;* or where he says, *unto each one of
us was the grace given according to the measure of the
gift of Christ* [3].   There were various grades and proportions in the prophetic gifts; and it is in contrast
to these that Christ is said to possess the gift *without
measure.*   .

Not only is there a difference of degree in the
insight which prophecy implied, but there is also an
evolution of its several parts, a progressive succession
in order of time.   Some things which belong to the
sphere of prophecy, such as the praise of the act of
Jael, the command for the extermination of the
Canaanites, what are called the 'imprecatory Psalms,'
were in place at one stage of the history of Revela-

---

[1] Jer. xlii. 7.   [2] 1 Cor. iii. ⅞ ⁵   [3] Eph. iv. 7.

tion, whereas they would not have been in place at
a later stage. It was in reference to such things as
these that our Lord rebuked the disciples by telling
them that they knew not *what spirit they were of*[1].
The disclosure of the Divine Will is gradual: it is
line upon line and precept upon precept ; one truth here
and another truth there, not all truth at once. The
description at the beginning of the Epistle to the
Hebrews emphatically holds good : Revelation was
given *at sundry times and in divers manners*, in many
portions and in many different forms.

When we turn from prophecy to the other great
elements in the Bible, to law and to history, to a certain extent the same phenomena meet us. It is the
prophetic spirit which is the proper vehicle of Revelation. And so far as both law and history contain a
revelation they too are prophetic. Moses is the first,
and in some ways perhaps the greatest, of the long
line of prophets. The historians were either prophets
themselves or wrote largely under the influence of
prophecy. It is this characteristic which has gained
them their place in the Bible. And so far as it is
embodied in them they would come under the same
laws, and the same principles would hold good in

[1] St. Luke ix. 55. Probably these words were really spoken by our
Lord, though they are wanting in so many of the best MSS. that they
can hardly have been part of the original Gospel : they seem to have
been added to it at a later but still early date from oral tradition.

respect to them as in respect to prophecy strictly so
called.

But in law and in history there was another ele-·
ment, which we may describe in a single word as
commemorative or historical. In regard to this
element different principles come into play. If we
take the historical Books and look at them no
longer as revelation but simply as history, then we
find ourselves on different ground. With the sacred
historians the record of fact as fact, and apart from
its significance in the unfolding of the Divine purpose,
is something very secondary and subordinate. Everything that bears on the Divine purpose, the religious
lessons to be drawn from the history, are pointed out
with great care and from a standpoint that is distinctly prophetic. But when once this prophetic
element is subtracted, the bare record of events which
remains does not seem to differ from any other
history. The writers tell us from what sources their
facts are derived just like any ordinary historian.
Even in the Pentateuch some ancient documents are
quoted like the 'Book of the Wars of the Lord [1],' or
the 'proverb' about Heshbon [2], and critical analysis
can detect the composite origin of the Books. When
we come to the Books of Samuel, Kings, and
Chronicles, the number of previous documents quoted
is greatly multiplied. The 'Book of Jashar,' or 'the

---

[1] Num. xxi. 14.   [2] Num. iv. 27–30.

Upright,' a collection of odes relating to the heroes
of Israel, the histories of Samuel, Gad, and Nathan—
perhaps, as it is thought, not three distinct works but
successive sections of a continuous single work—the
'acts' of Solomon, the 'chronicles' of the kings of Israel
and of the kings of Judah both separately and combined, 'commentaries' like those of Iddo the prophet[1],
the 'acts' of Uzziah which had no less an author than
Isaiah[2], and another work by the same prophet dealing with the reign of Hezekiah[3]—all these and more
are enumerated as authorities, just as any profane
historian might refer to the sources from which he
was drawing. These various documents vary also in
value; some are very near and even contemporary
with the events, some are separated by a greater or
less interval from them. A large proportion of the
narratives, especially in the earlier books, must rest
ultimately upon oral tradition, committed to writing
after a considerable lapse of time. I know of nothing
which would mark off these merely as narratives
from others of the same kind outside the Bible.
I know of nothing which should isolate them, and
prevent us from judging them as we should other
similar narratives. Their authority must needs rise
or fall according to the relation of the writer to the
events : some will rank higher, some lower : some will

[1] 2 Chron. xiii. 22.   [2] 2 Chron. xxvi. 22.
[3] 2 Chron. xxxii. 32.

carry with them better attestation than others. But so far as the Bible itself instructs us on the point, I do not see how we can claim for them a strict immunity from error. There is indeed a gradual shading off. Some parts of the Old Testament stand out as unique and distinct from all other books ; others, so far as we can judge, are on much the same level with them.

We turn to the New Testament and we find there phenomena of much the same kind. St. Paul lets us see plainly what his inspiration is, and how far it extends. The passage quoted on the last occasion is decisive as to the central features at least in his teaching: he did not receive it from man, neither was he taught it, but it came to him through revelation of Jesus Christ. The person of St. Paul is surrounded by the supernatural. Through all the modes in which the Spirit of God held communion with the elder prophets, the same Divine influences were communicated to him. He too prophesied; he spake with tongues ; he received intimations of the Divine Will in dreams, in visions, in other ways not more particularly specified. But yet he too not only drew the distinctions, to which reference has been already made, between the different degrees of inspiration vouchsafed to different individuals, but he was also conscious of degrees in his own inspiration and in the authority with which he spoke on different occasions.

This comes out clearly in the chapter which contains so much wise counsel on the subject of marriage[1]. For one of his precepts he claims an authority higher than his own: *unto the married I give charge, yet not I but the Lord*[2]. For another he will not claim so much as this: *to the rest say I, not the Lord*[3]. Other precepts he places rather upon the footing of advice than of command. *Concerning virgins,* he says, *I have no commandment of the Lord: but I give my judgment, as one that hath obtained mercy of the Lord to be faithful*[4]; where the word 'judgment' means rather the decision to which he has come in his own mind, than anything which he regarded as binding upon others; it is only a little stronger than 'opinion.' Again, at the end of the chapter, speaking of a widow, he says: *she is happier if she abide as she is, after my judgment: and I think that I also have the Spirit of God*[5]. The Apostle modestly claims for himself some enlightenment from above, but still he will not press his opinion with too much emphasis. He does not regard it as an absolute law for all Christians. It happens that the Apostle does not elsewhere graduate his precepts in the same explicit manner, but we can well believe that he did so tacitly.

In the New Testament as in the Old there is the

---

[1] I Cor. vii.   [2] *Ibid.* 10.   [3] *Ibid.* 12.
[4] *Ibid.* 25.   [5] *Ibid.* 40.

same sort of difference between doctrine and history. Where the history contains doctrine, there we have every reason to suppose that the doctrine rests upon the same supernatural basis, that it is as intimately connected with the great Messianic outpouring of the Spirit as it is elsewhere. But the history *as* history, as a narrative of events, appears to proceed upon ordinary methods. The classical passage for this is the preface to the Gospel of St. Luke. Here the Evangelist writes just like any other historian. He claims that his narrative is based upon the report of eye-witnesses, and the attendants and helpers of eye-witnesses : he claims to have used all possible care and research : but he nowhere assumes supernatural direction : he apparently wishes to have his work taken upon its merits. We are quite prepared to find that he has made use of pre-existing materials. And, as a matter of fact, when the Gospel and the Acts come to be closely examined, there is strong reason to believe that both works have incorporated in them the contents of older documents. We are reminded that there is a criticism of the New Testament as well as of the Old. And this criticism has made considerable progress, though a final result has not yet been arrived at. One of the chief subjects of debate is the composition of the first three Gospels. These can no longer be treated as so many independent witnesses to the same events.

It is far more probable that the common element
in them is all derived from a single source, whether
that source were in writing, or whether it represents
a common body of oral tradition. I would only
remark in passing that if we lose in thus having
only one ultimate witness instead of three, we gain
in that this one witness is thrown back to a date
anterior to the three which have come down to us,
and is so brought still nearer to the events, with
a corresponding increase in its value as history.

In the Book of Acts in like manner older sources
of information appear to have been used. But otherwise, except that the Epistle to the Hebrews is now
usually assigned to some other writer than St. Paul,
and that the evidence for 2 St. Peter[1] is acknow-
ledged to be inferior to that for the other books,

---

[1] Doing my best to weigh impartially the arguments for and against
2 St. Peter, I do not find myself able to get beyond a *non liquet*: if the
arguments in its favour are unconvincing, so also are those on the other
side. The defective external attestation ; the (probable) use of St.
Jude ; the strangeness of diction and alleged coincidences with Josephus ;
the reference to the delay of the Second Coming—are not incompatible
with the genuineness of the Epistle. One of the strongest points is
perhaps the designation of St. Paul's Epistles as γραφαί. But it is certain that in the first century this term was not confined to the Books of
the Hebrew Canon : and I am not clear that it might not be applied at
an early date to works possessing such high prophetic authority as the
Epistles of St. Paul. Already, in the year 57, we see what an impression these Epistles had made from 2 Cor. x. 10. We hesitate, too,
to treat quite so freely as if it were anonymous an Epistle which bears
the name of St. Peter distinctly upon its front, and at the same time

there is less clear reason for revising the traditional
verdicts upon the Books of the New Testament than
on those of the Old.   The Books most impugned are
St. John's Gospel (and Epistles) and the Pastoral
Epistles.   Others of the Epistles are criticized, and
a new theory has recently been put forward about
the Apocalypse.   But in none of these cases has the
innovating theory been proved at all conclusively [1].

I must not go further into these details, but must
attempt to sum up briefly the results at which we
seem to arrive.   What is the relation of the natural
to the supernatural, of the human to the Divine,
in the Bible?   They shade off into each other by
almost insensible degrees ; but at the two ends of the
scale they are wide enough apart to stand out quite
clearly.   In all that relates to the Revelation of God
and of His Will, the writers assert for themselves

gives no sign of disingenuous motive. On the whole question I am
much inclined to adopt the able summing-up given by Dr. Salmon
(*Introd.* pp. 529–559, ed. 4).

[1] To say this is not to deny that there are some points in these
writings which are imperfectly explained with our present knowledge.
Our German friends, as a rule, seem to me to allow too small a margin
for possibilities due simply to our ignorance. Bearing these in mind
the *balance* of argument seems to me in the main clear on the side of
tradition. The freaks of criticism of which something has been heard
of late in Holland and Switzerland are mere extravagances, which only
serve to put us on our guard against the kind of arguments relied upon.
The most decisive reply is probably that by Gloël, *Die jüngste Kritik
des Galaterbriefes*, Erlangen and Leipzig, 1890. Dr. Gloël is a writer
with whom I find myself in much agreement.

a definite inspiration; they claim to speak with an authority higher than their own. But in regard to the narrative of events, and to processes of literary composition, there is nothing so exceptional about them as to exempt them from the conditions to which other works would be exposed at the same place and time.

St. Peter compares the light of prophecy to that of a lamp shining in a dark place ; our Lord compared the Kingdom of Heaven in all its many aspects to *leaven hid in three measures of meal.* The light of a lamp has a vivid centre with a corona which melts by degrees into the darkness by which it is surrounded. The leaven in the lump of dough ferments at first most actively at the point at which it is inserted. In both cases there is an active force introduced into material which offers some resistance to it. So is it with Revelation : the heavenly and the earthly mix and blend. Human instruments are made use of for Divine ends. The humanity is not lost : it is not even altogether transfigured : but it performs its office none the less. It is the medium through which the knowledge of God is imparted to ever-widening circles among the sons of men.

VI.

LOSS AND GAIN.

(Whitehall, August 10, 1890.)

ISAIAH xi. 9.

The earth shall be full of the knowledge of the Lord, as the waters cover the sea.

WE are now perhaps in a position to estimate rather more closely the effect which the changes of which we have been speaking are likely to have upon the faith of Christians. It must be admitted frankly that they involve a loss. They make the intellectual side of the connexion between Christian belief and Christian practice a matter of greater difficulty than it has hitherto seemed to be. In old days it was very much as with the Jews in the time of our Lord. When any question arose of doctrine or practice, all that was needed was to turn the pages of Scripture until one came to a place which bore upon the point at issue. This was at once applied just as it stood, without hesitation and without misgiving. It becomes a different matter when the enquirer feels bound not only to take the passage along with its context, but also to ask who was the author, when did he write, and with what stage in the history of Revelation is the particular utterance connected? Really the difference is not in principle at least so great as it seems, because in all ages it has been recognised that there were some things in the Bible, and especially in the Old Testament, which could not be transferred just as they stood to a later day. For instance, no one in Christian times would have thought of justifying the practice of polygamy by the examples of the Patriarchs and Kings of Israel. And for more than one generation past, in this country at least, no one would have thought of finding a similar justification for the institution of Slavery. In principle, therefore, the two points of view are the same, and what appears to be a change is only the extension to other and less obvious places of a rule which had been already recognised implicitly, if not explicitly, in regard to a few that were more obvious. Increased knowledge, in this as in other things, brings with it increased responsibilities; and if more is required of the present generation than was required of our fathers, the facilities put in their hands are also far greater. The general level of education has been raised ; books are multiplied, and in the next few years may be expected to multiply still more, and to improve in quality—at least so far as quality means the diffusion of special knowledge hitherto in the hands of a few—

even more than in quantity. There is besides this
consolation. The main outlines of Christian faith
and Christian duty are well understood independently
of the interpretation of particular passages. They
have entered into the life of the Church as a whole,
and are handed on from age to age. The plain man
who studies his Bible within the limits imposed by
these cannot very well go wrong. And there is the
incidental but great advantage that in proportion as
the average of Biblical knowledge rises it will become
more and more impossible to split up the Church into
the multitude of small and eccentric sects which have
hitherto been so disastrous to it. A few broad lines
of division will no doubt remain, but many of the
minor varieties will probably be absorbed, while it is
hardly possible that their number can be increased.
Perverse and sectional interpretations of the Scriptures will not be able to live in the future as they
have done in the past in the face of an instructed
public opinion. As knowledge widens, all classes of
society will move together more than they have done.
We may look to have a larger *consensus* of opinion,
and along with it a greater readiness to join in con-
certed action.

When we have said that the use which good men
will make of the Bible may be expected to become
less simple and less definite in its details, that it will
involve more research and more trouble, and that less

educated Christians will perhaps pay more deference
to the opinion of the more educated and to the
advancing consciousness of the Church at large, we
shall, I think, have said all that need be said as to
the loss—surely not all loss—for which we must be
prepared. But if we assign the utmost weight to
this, it will, I think, be far more than counterbalanced
by the gain.

The first gain is a gain in truth. I do not wish to
assume the ultimate establishment of any particular
set of propositions. All that I mean is that those
which are ultimately established—those which obtain
a large amount of general acceptance—will do so
because they are true. There is great force in the
old adage, *Securus judicat orbis terrarum*, ' The
whole world can't go wrong.' Only we should of
course take this in its literal sense, and not confine it
to a particular section of the world which happens to
assume to itself a special infallibility. For practical
purposes, a Christian means by the world in this connexion the great mass of Christian opinion. Happily
this is now becoming a much more real thing than it
was. Theology is becoming far more international
and interconfessional. England and France are joining
hands with Germany, and America[1] is joining hands

---

[1] The rise of theological scholarship (as distinct from dogmatic
or philosophical theology) in America may be said to date from Professors Andrews Norton, of Harvard (died 1853), and Moses Stuart, of

with England. Lutheran scholars and Reformed
Anglican and Presbyterian are all making common
cause. And even Roman Catholics do not hold
aloof[1]. Men are comparing notes the whole world
over, and extravagances and aberrations are being
struck off on this side and on that. Before this great
tribunal, eccentricities cannot stand. Some public
man, I forget who, is reported to have said that 'all
sensible men were of one religion.' The saying was a
bold one at the time when it was uttered : it would
still be bold, and an anticipation of a perhaps distant
future. But this at least we may say : that an agreement upon the critical bases of religion is far more
within sight than it was even a short time ago. There
is a more reasonable temper all round. Men are
beginning to ask in what they can agree with as

Andover (died 1852). Professor Norton left a distinguished follower
in Dr. Ezra Abbot (died 1884). Biblical and theological studies
flourish at the present moment under Dr. Thayer at Harvard, Dr.
Dwight and Dr. Fisher of Yale; Dr. Schaff, Dr. Briggs, and Dr.
Isaac Hall at New York; Dr. Green and Dr. Warfield at Princeton;
and Professor Rendel Harris (who is English by birth and training) at
Haverford College, Pennsylvania.

[1] Besides the Old Catholics like Dr. Döllinger, so lately taken away,
Bishop Reinkens and Professors Reusch and Friedrich, there is an
admirable school at Paris at the head of which is the Abbé Duchesne—
one of the first theological scholars in Europe,—M. Le Blant, M.
Tixeront, and the Abbé Batiffol: in Germany, Bishop Hefele, Professors Kraus, Funk, and Schanz; in Rome, Cardinal Hergenröther
and the veteran De Rossi, who in 1885 lost the companionship of
another distinguished Christian archaeologist, Garrucci.

much willingness as to fight the points on which they differ. This is a good augury, and one which is every day pronouncing itself more clearly.

The next gain is a gain in security. Belief which rests on grounds such as I have been describing touches the bottom; it feels the solid rock. Belief which rests upon authority has always a certain amount of scaffolding between it and the base on which it stands; and the mind cannot help being haunted by the doubt whether that scaffolding is strong and firm enough to bear the weight thrown upon it. Will the authority itself bear the solvents of criticism? But belief which has been itself tested by criticism—which comes out as the result of a critical process — cannot have any further solvent applied to it. Its anchor cannot drag. Its roots go down into the very constitution of the human mind. And the faith which springs from it has all that buoyancy and sense of freedom which comes from having no reserve—no weak place which one shrinks from putting to the proof. The confidence which comes from the rigorous exclusion of opposing forces is one thing: that which comes from having met and fought and conquered them is another. The last alone is a healthy confidence; it alone carries with it the true assurance and elation of victory.

A third gain is the gain in reality. The old way of looking at the Bible was mainly as a collection of

G

doctrines—a number of abstract propositions which might indeed be *applied* to life, but which were not themselves in any full sense living. The new way makes them live and breathe so intensely that their life cannot help being communicated even across the gulf of ages. It is like the story of Elisha, who we are told went up and lay upon the dead child, *and put his mouth upon his mouth and his eyes upon his eyes and his hands upon his hands; and he stretched himself upon the child, and the flesh of the child waxed warm* [1]. Such is the contact into which our modern im-poverished existence is brought with the ancient and perennial spring of life contained in the Bible. By treating the Bible history as a human history like any other, by investing each period and stage in it with all the surroundings proper to that period, by observing the close and intimate relation which doctrine always bears to the times and circumstances out of which it arises, the doctrine itself acquires a new vitality. An ideal, however high, when severed from life, has always something thin and pale and in-effective about it. Take the same ideal and find a body for it; infuse into it a touch of genuine realism ; let it be seen how it glows through its veil of flesh, how it courses like pure blood through the arteries, how it puts its own fine lines upon the features and kindles them with its own enthusiasm, and it becomes

[1] 2 Kings iv. 34.

tenfold more winning and attractive—not only inspired itself but a source of real inspiration in others.
St. Paul speaks of Christians *reflecting as in a mirror
the glory of the Lord, being transformed into the same
image from glory to glory* [1], and that should be the case
with all who are brought into vital and vitalizing
contact with the Bible.

Truth, security, reality are three things closely
allied to each other. They are only different aspects
of the result of a more profound study, a more
thorough apprehension of the Bible *as it is* and not
as we imagine it to be. The gain which they represent is one for which it would not be easy to pay
too dear. Of course I do not mean that we shall
grasp the whole amount of this gain all at once.
This too, like all other processes, must be gradual.
But it is a process on which, as it seems to me, we
are well launched. The Continent is ahead of us
just at present: in Germany especially the results of
criticism have been more fully assimilated: but I
believe that we shall soon do more than make up
for lost time, as the scholars of our own, in whose
hands the working out of these problems lies, are
distinguished by a peculiarly happy balance between
the interests of religion and of science: we may be
sure that the one will not be sacrificed to the other.

There is, however, another point which I think

[1] 2 Cor. iii. 18.

G 2

that we need not hesitate to set down under the head
of 'gain,' in the change involved in the manner of
using the Bible. Hitherto the use which has been
made of it has been mainly of two kinds. On the
one hand it has been taken as the basis of formulated
doctrine, such as constitutes the substance of Creeds
and Articles. On the other hand single texts have
been constantly applied as sources of stimulus or of
comfort. The last is the use which has been most
common with plain, everyday Christians ; the first is
that which has exercised the leaders of Christian
thought and the deliberations of the great Church
assemblies. Both these uses are legitimate, and ought
not to be disparaged. Only it is not wrong to bear in
mind that, while the decisions of Councils, representing as they do the deliberate judgment of the great
majority of the Church at moments when a clear
issue has been set before it, are not likely to be
reversed,—so that, for instance, it is extremely im-
probable that anything at all corresponding to the
Arianism which was rejected in the fourth century
should establish itself in the nineteenth or twentieth,—
these decisions are nevertheless historical in their
character, having relation to particular phases of
thought prevailing at particular periods, and therefore are apt to lose, if not their essential truth, yet
to some extent their interest and appositeness to
the present. With this qualification the two older

uses of the Bible will ·doubtless continue, and need
not be called in question. But there is yet a third
use which it seems to me is likely to become more
and more prominent in the future: I mean, the use
of the Bible not merely as a basis for abstract
doctrine, more or less metaphysical, and not merely
in the form of isolated single texts directly applied
to the life of individuals, but in a form which might
be described as standing midway between these, and
more in accordance with the circumstances under
which the Biblical revelations were originally communicated. What, when we come to think of it, was the
method of those revelations? They were not primarily
metaphysics or pure abstractions, neither were they a
collection of detailed maxims or aphorisms, but they
consisted of certain great ruling principles or ideas,
always enunciated in connexion with some pressing
problem of actual practical life, and usually on a
somewhat large scale. Let me enumerate some of
these ruling ideas or principles, so that I may be better
understood. The Fatherhood of God is one of them,
an idea realized—or that ought to be realized—by
Jew and Christian with a force and in a degree un-
imagined, I believe I am right in saying, by any
people outside the sphere of our own special Revelation ; the Holiness, and yet more, the Loving-kind-
ness of God, an idea which, again, has nowhere
reached anything like the intensity of expression

which it has attained in the Jewish Prophets and in Christianity; the Kingdom, or I would say rather the Reign, of God, not merely in the form of an earthly society, but more searching and pervasive in its action ; the Divine Choice, both of individuals and of nations, to be the instruments of God's mighty purposes, with the corresponding idea so prominent, first in Isaiah and then in St. Paul, of the preservation of a faithful Remnant in times of trial and apostasy; the great and dominant idea which runs through both Old and New Testament, from the beginning to the end of the Divinely-wrought Deliverance or Deliverances culminating in the Redemption of Christ ; and along with this another leading idea, which again passes in a deeper and more penetrating sense from the Old Testament to the New, of the Indwelling of God among His people ; and yet once more the idea on which this last is based, of the relation as of Covenant into which God enters with His Chosen, in its twofold aspect as implying at once privileges and obligations.

All these it will be felt are something more than ideas ; they are *moving* ideas or *forces*; they appeal, when rightly presented, not only to the intellect but to the emotions; they do not only guide and direct, but they add elevation, strength, buoyancy to life. They are that Divine element which is capable of counteracting the wear and tear, the troubles, anxieties, and sorrows, the weaknesses and temptations of this earthly existence.

It would of course be an absurd exaggeration to say that the ideas or principles or forces, of which I have been speaking, have not hitherto played their part in Christianity. Every one who reads his Bible at all must recognise their presence. At particular periods in history first one and then another has been brought into special prominence. But the way in which this has been done has not been quite happy. There has been too much of a tendency to erect them into abstract dogmas. That was not the form in which they were first promulgated, but as living, pulsating, moving truths, which came from the lips of Prophets and Apostles with genuine inspiration, and which carried their inspiring power with them wherever they penetrated. I cannot help thinking that the critical and historical way of looking at the Bible is calculated to win back some of this inspiring power. It takes them out of the region of abstractions and puts them again into relation with life. But life is the true generator of life. Let us see the fabric of Divine Revelation rising up around us as it really rose; let us see its different parts one after another in contact with the actual crises of history; let us observe them working like leaven in some of the strongest, grandest, richest of human personalities—an Isaiah or a St. Paul; let

us observe them swaying the fortunes of nations and
masses of men ; let us mark how the light first dawns
and then broadens ; how the formative force which
God has implanted in His Revelation draws into its
vortex, absorbs and assimilates first this and then
that element of extraneous or secular culture ; let
us trace the mighty purpose which runs through
the ages down even to our own time ; and it seems
to me that both our hearts and our imaginations
must be kindled and inflamed to the very utmost
of their capacity.   It is not for me to find fault with
the work of men who as preachers and teachers
have far greater gifts than my own, but I cannot help
thinking that there has been something rather half-
hearted in the presentation of what I believe to be
the real fundamentals of Christianity, and all for
want of that vital apprehension of them which should
be the proper fruit of criticism and history.   We
have played too long upon the surface of things : but
the time is coming I believe—thanks to that movement which has filled some with a natural but mistaken alarm—when we shall be so possessed with
these great truths ourselves, that we shall be able
to convey more of their greatness to others.   The
Christian who studies the signs of the times will not
despond, but he will rather look up and lift up his
head, for, in spite of the clouds which drift fitfully
across his vision, the sky is really bright above him.

VII.

TRUE AND FALSE INSPIRATION.

(Exeter College Chapel, Oct. 26, 1890.)

JEREMIAH v. 30, 31.

A wonderful and horrible thing is come to pass in the land; the prophets prophesy falsely, and the priests bear rule by their means; and my people love to have it so: and what will ye do in the end thereof?

THE Christian who rests his belief in the Bible primarily upon the Bible itself—who finds that nothing impresses him so strongly as the conviction which the Biblical writers themselves evidently had that their words were an announcement of the Divine Will and were put in their hearts by the Holy Spirit —will find himself confronted with two questions : (1) How is he to tell where this Divine prompting begins and where it ends, in other words, what is inspired and what is not ? and (2) How is he to distinguish true inspiration from false ?

The first question will not trouble him very greatly. All he has to do is to pursue the same method with which he began—to look closely at the language which the Biblical writers use, and to see where they claim inspiration and where they do not, where they profess to speak the words of God, and where they write after the manner of other men. This is a line of thought which any one can work out for himself. I have spoken about it elsewhere[1], and I do not intend to return to it now. But the other question needs, I think, to be more directly dealt with. I am not sure that it is not the last fundamental question on this side which a theology which seeks to build itself up without assumptions has to ask.

Again we have not to look outside the Bible for a hint of its own limitations. I have pointed out on other occasions that the essence of the Bible lies in prophecy. The prophetic spirit is the proper vehicle of revelation. This holds good for the New Testament equally with the Old, for St. Paul and St. John are as much prophets as Isaiah and Hosea. But if this is so—and I may perhaps for the present assume without staying to prove it—then it is distinctly recognised all through the Bible that there are false prophets and false prophecy side by side with the true. We need to remember that prophecy was a profession, and that the prophets formed a professional class. There were schools of the prophets in which the gift was regularly cultivated. A group of young men would gather round some commanding figure—a Samuel or an Elisha—and would not only

[1] See Lecture V.

record or spread the knowledge of his sayings and doings, but seek to catch themselves something of his inspiration. It seems that music played its part in their exercises [1]. It was not, however, necessary to belong to one of these schools in order to be a prophet. The prophet Amos tells us expressly that he was no prophet, neither was he a prophet's son [2], where prophet's son means practically the same thing as 'member of a society,' like that certain man of the sons of the prophets [3] who gave a sign to Ahab condemning him for sparing the life of Ben-hadad. And on the other hand it is perfectly clear that by no means all of these sons of the prophets ever succeeded in acquiring more than a very small share in the gift which they sought. It was clearly possible to 'counterfeit' prophecy. Sometimes that was done deliberately, as in the case of the deception practised upon the man of God who was sent to speak against the altar of Jeroboam at Bethel [4]. But it by no means follows that in all cases where a false message was given the giver of it was altogether conscious of what he was doing. Every one will remember that striking scene at the end of the First Book of Kings [5] where Ahab and Jehoshaphat gather together the prophets, about 400 in number, to enquire whether or not they are to go up against

[1] 1 Samuel x. 5.   [2] Amos vii. 14.   [3] 1 Kings xx. 35.
[4] 1 Kings xiii. 18.   [5] 1 Kings xxii.

the Syrians at Ramoth-Gilead, and how, when
the king of Israel puts to them the question,
with one voice they encourage him to go, one of
the prophets in the approved prophetic fashion
making himself horns of iron to symbolize the defeat
which would be inflicted on the Syrians. Jehoshaphat
is not perfectly satisfied, and he asks if there is not
besides a prophet of Jehovah. With some reluctance
Micaiah is produced, though Ahab confesses that he
hates him. Micaiah prophesies the death of the
king, and *Israel scattered like sheep that have no
shepherd.* He goes on to explain by a parable the
unanimity of his opponents. He had seen *the Lord
sitting on His throne with the host of heaven on the
right hand and on the left.* The question was proposed how Ahab was to be persuaded to go up
and fall at Ramoth-Gilead, and at last one of the
spirits offers to *go forth and be a lying spirit in
the mouth of all his prophets.* The offer is accepted
and the mission succeeds[1]. We can see from the
context how there are mixed motives at work. The
400 prophets truckle to the powerful monarch, who
is impatient of anything which does not run in the
direction of his own wishes. But on the other hand
there is a *spirit of delusion* abroad as well. We
are not to suppose that these men really knew that
Ahab would fall : their minds were warped by self-

[1] 1 Kings xxii. 17–23.

interest, and they deceived themselves before they deceived others.

In every age of the Church a very broad distinction must be drawn between the machinery of revelation or of spiritual influence and the revelation or spiritual influence itself. Nothing can be more decisive on this head than the verses from the Book of Jeremiah which I took as my text. The prophet looks out upon the theocracy as it was in his day, and he sees that every part of it is corrupt : the whole organization is out of gear; *the prophets prophesy falsely;* the priests are set on their own power and advancement ; the people know that things are wrong and yet they will not insist on amendment ; they would rather have smooth things and peace and comfort than brace themselves for any strenuous effort at reform. So *the whole head is sick and the whole heart faint.* Religion itself is poisoned at its source.

A passage like this is an emphatic warning to all times. It is no doubt an extreme state of things. Jeremiah himself is conscious that it is. He calls it *a wonderful and horrible thing.* But tendencies are best seen by extremes. It does not follow that because there are prophets all is truth, or because there are priests all is righteousness and holiness.

This then is one part of the problem before us. How are we to distinguish true from false inspiration

—how are we to distinguish it within the sphere of
Revelation itself? And another part of it is, How
are we to distinguish one professing revelation from
another? I cannot bring myself—and there is really
nothing in the history of Christianity to compel me
to bring myself—to divide religions absolutely into
true and false. From the first days of Christian
teaching down to our own there has been not wanting
a succession of men who have seen and rejoiced
in the elements of good in Creeds which we have
not subscribed. Take a phenomenon like the oracle
at Delphi; take that most touching account which
Plato gives of the δαιμόνιον of Socrates; take the
teaching of Gautama (Buddha); analyse the character
of Mahomet;—shall we say that there is no 'spark
from heaven' in these? Assuredly there are 'sparks
from heaven'—assuredly there are 'seeds of the
Divine Word' (σπέρματα τοῦ Λόγου)—assuredly there
were (as Justin Martyr recognised) 'Christians before
Christ'—assuredly even now there are 'heathen who
are not heathen'—*not My people* who shall be called
My people, and *not beloved* who shall be called
Beloved[1]. We may be asked then what account we
give of these. What test should we apply? What
is the bearing of the existence of false prophecy in
Israel upon the religion of the Bible? How are we to
correlate that religion with the ethnic religions?

[1] Romans ix. 25; Hosea ii. 23.

In the first place let us weigh this simple fact. The Bible speaks of false prophets even in Israel. But no one would say that the Bible itself contained false prophecy—for false prophecy and unfulfilled prophecy are not the same thing. False prophecy might have its place in Israel; but it had no rightful place in the religion of Israel. The words of the Law are most emphatic: *The prophet which shall speak a word presumptuously in my name, which I have not commanded him to speak, or that shall speak in the name of other gods, that same prophet shall die*[1]. The safeguard against false prophecy has been the Canon of Scripture. A process of sifting has taken place. If we look at it from one point of view we may call the efficient cause the Providence of God: if we look at it from another point of view we may call it the consciousness of the Church. It has been agreed to mark off certain books from others as containing in a special sense the Word of God. I will not take upon myself to say that the verdict of the past may not conceivably undergo revision. It has already been to a certain extent revised—at the Reformation : and two different estimates are current in the Roman and in the Reformed Churches. It is possible that the future may have in store for us another such revision. No doubt points are present to people's minds now which were not equally present

[1] Deut. xviii. 20.

in the early ages. These points might perhaps be
taken into fuller consideration. But at present there
does not seem to be any inclination even among those
who question the dates and authorship of some of the
books to displace them as Scripture. The most
would seem to be that some of the books (e. g.
2 St. Peter) are appealed to as authorities with rather
more hesitation than others. Taken as a whole it
may be said that the verdict of the later Church has
ratified the verdict of the earlier. Christendom still
holds that the truths for which Prophets and Apostles
contended are really truths—and truths which are not
unworthy to have been revealed from above. In this
we may well see a Divine guidance. But indeed the
process by which the Canon was formed gave the
best guarantee of permanence. It is based upon an
instinct which went deeper than argument. The
'usage of the Churches' was better than any
theoretical criteria. Those books were adopted which
possessed the same credentials as the Apostles
possessed, and which proved themselves to be divine
by the *demonstration of the Spirit and of power.*

That is our answer to those who ask what means
we have of discriminating pretended revelation from
true. And our answer is not dissimilar to those who
ask how we weigh the claims of prophetic manifesta-
tions in Greece, or Arabia, or India, as compared with
those in Israel or that wider 'spiritual Israel' which

we call Christianity. In the perspective of history, truth and falsehood, lower truth and higher truth, disentangle themselves, and stand out with quite sufficient clearness. *Vicisti Galilaee* are the dying words attributed to the last imperial champion of Paganism, and the Muse of history does but take them up and echo them. Let us deny nothing, let us depreciate and minimize nothing of all that there is of high and unworldly aspiration, of all that there is of deep and penetrating insight in the religions external to Christianity. The facts are there, and it is our duty to accept and rejoice over them. They are the outskirts of the working of that Divine Spirit which fills the universe. But because we recognise this we do not therefore touch the prerogative of our own religion. Let us take two examples out of those which have been mentioned. One of the most striking things about Socrates is what he calls his ' Daemon,' that voice which has attended him from his youth up and whispers in his ear when he or those in whom he is interested are about to do anything that they should not. It is a pathetic touch, when, in the Epilogue to his Apology, he consoles those who voted for his acquittal by telling them that this Warning Voice of his, which in all the rest of his life had been ready enough to stop him when he was doing anything wrong or unpropitious, placed no obstacle before him when he went out to his arrest,

H

or when he was on his way to trial, or at any part of
his speech in his own defence. At other times it was
in the habit of interrupting him while he was speaking, but it had not done so then. He argued from
this that it was a mistake to suppose that death was
an evil. Otherwise his mentor would not have let
him go to certain death [1].

Again, if we take the case of Mahomet, a just
criticism must see in him an element—and even a
large element—of sincerity. He really felt himself
called to be the prophet of God, to preach that God
was one, that idols were nought, that absolute sub-
mission to God's will was the first duty of man.
These were real truths, descended in fact from
Judaism, and to be conscious of a commission to
proclaim them was no imposture. But unfortunately
this is not the only element in Mahometanism. There
is too much in that religion—too much in the Koran—
which was dictated, not by any genuine inspiration,
but by the prophet's own strong passions [2].

Neither Socrates nor Mahomet afford more than
a very rudimentary and imperfect analogy to the
Bible. Delightful as is the simplicity with which the

---

[1] Plato, *Apol. Socr.* c. 31 (p. 40).

[2] It is a pleasure to refer once more to Dr. Dale's book, where
the case of Mahometanism is also considered in connexion with an
argument similar to that of Lecture III, and treated as it seems
to me very directly and satisfactorily. See *The Living Christ*, &c.
pp. 64–68.

Platonic Socrates speaks of his familiar spirit, so free from strain and assumption, and with just a touch of playfulness which softens but does not conceal the seriousness of character in which the conception has its rise, the Daemon is after all only a negative thing. It checks and dissuades, but it does no more[1]. The beautiful argument about death is only suggested by its prompting[2]. And when we compare the Koran with the Bible, the disinterestedness, the richness and fulness of the latter stand out more than ever. What is best in the Koran is only reflected from the Bible. And how much is there in the Bible to which the Koran affords no parallel! How powerful is that stream of enlightenment and truth which grows broader and deeper, and gains at every stage in volume and force, as prophet succeeds prophet, and the Law makes way for the Gospel!

In putting the religion of the Bible at the head of all religions, in claiming for its exponents a real Divine inspiration, we do not take it out of all natural conditions. Inspiration works through human faculties: it does not supersede them. The analogies which connect Biblical religion with other religions are not all illusory. Healthy phenomena pass into

---

[1] This is the description which Socrates is made to give of it: ἔστι γάρ τι θείᾳ μοίρᾳ παρεπόμενον ἐμοὶ ἐκ παιδὸς ἀρξάμενον δαιμόνιον, ἔστι δὲ τοῦτο φωνή, ἣ ὅταν γένηται, ἀεί μοι σημαίνει, ὃ ἂν μέλλω πράττειν, τούτου ἀποτροπήν, προτρέπει δὲ οὐδέποτε. Plato, *Theages*, c. 11 (p. 128).

[2] *Apol. Socr.* c. 31 (p. 40).

morbid, lower into higher, natural into supernatural, by the most gradual transitions. It is a mistake to set the natural and the supernatural in too sharp antithesis. Whether we look at the individual who is endowed with the prophetic gift and study the process by which that gift receives expression, or whether we look at the whole complex product of prophetic religion, they touch each other all along the line, and it is equally difficult to say where the one ends and the other begins. Perhaps it is well that we should be reminded in this way that both are really parts of the same great Divine economy. They proceed from the same Author; they co-operate for the same ends; they are included in the same vast chain of causation. The only difference is that we know a little more about the one than we do about the other, and that the Power which presides over both alike lays—or seems to lay—a little more stress here than He does there. When the organist sits at the key-board of his instrument he plays some passages soft and some loud; sometimes the notes that he gives forth are muffled, sometimes they are loud and clear. But the different parts of his playing are all upon the same instrument, and they all harmonize together. The very same note is alternately subdued and emphasized; and there are *crescendoes* and *diminuendoes* to connect the soft with the loud. So with Him who sits at the key-board of the universe, and touches now with lighter and now with more constraining force the chords of the human spirit : the music which results is not broken and discordant, but it all blends into a subtle harmony and the rising and the falling cadences alike contribute to the whole.

VIII.

CHRIST AND' THE SCRIPTURES.

(Exeter College Chapel, Nov. 9, 1890.)

HEBREWS ii. 7.

Thou madest Him a little lower than the angels.

THE controversy respecting the criticism of the Old Testament has taken what I cannot but think a very unfortunate turn.   The true method in this and in all cognate questions seems to me to be first, at all costs of time and labour, to ascertain what are the exact facts.   When that has been done the explanation of the facts will come almost of itself.   We shall see them in their true proportions, and they will fall into their proper place and relation to each other. It is the reverse of this to take a single text, to draw from it at once far-reaching dogmatic consequences and so to foreclose by an appeal to authority the whole line of detailed investigations.   It is needless to say that even the effect which is sought will not be attained.   The investigations will go on all the same.   And meanwhile they will be conducted under prejudice on both sides, and when they have reached their conclusion the shock of collision between the opposed opinions will be all the greater.

It does not however follow because I would deprecate this that I would have us shrink from facing any question that may be legitimately proposed to us. In this particular instance it is not so much the raising of the question that I deprecate as the time and place, the logical order, in which it is raised, and the use that is made of it in controversy. Sooner or later we must no doubt be clear in our own minds as to the bearing of certain quotations from the Old Testament in the Gospels. The question involved is nothing less than the authority of our Lord Himself. His authority is thought to sanction the traditional views as to the origin and authorship of the Books of the Old Testament, and to preclude from the outset the adoption of any other.

There is therefore a distinct issue placed before us which we must not decline because we would rather take it in a different order or because we hesitate to touch a point on which misunderstanding is so easy. Happily this last danger is greatly lightened for those who are committed to the cause of criticism by the wise and thoughtful utterances of leaders in the Church who are not so committed[1]. Never, as it

[1] I have in my mind not only the publicly expressed opinions of the Archbishop of Canterbury and the Bishops of Carlisle, Durham, and Oxford, but even more, those of the Bishop of Lincoln and Dr. Gregory

seems to me, has a great and really momentous question been approached from all sides in so excellent a
temper.

I venture then, with a prayer for chastened and
careful speech, to address myself to it this evening.

In some positions he who would climb a perilous
ascent seeks to plant his feet firm before he makes
another forward motion. Let us do this by first re-
calling to our minds why it is that we invest every
word spoken by our Lord with such supreme authority. We regard His words as the words of One who
was God as well as Man. And we so regard them,
I think it may be said, for three reasons : (1) because
of the way in which He spoke about Himself; (2)
because of the impression which He made upon His
companions and contemporaries, notably such men
as St. Paul and St. Peter and St. John ; (3) because
of the prolonged and tried experience of the Church
at large.

(1) In order to have unimpeachable standing-ground,
I reserve expressions, such as those in the Fourth
Gospel, which might be thought to bear witness
rather to the intense conviction of the disciple than
to the certain affirmation of the Master, and I confine myself to the Synoptic Gospels. There we have

Smith. Where men of such delicate and sensitive loyalty have gone
before it is far easier for others to follow: the edge is taken from
criticism when its course is guided by such hands.

a number of mysterious claims which are all the
more impressive because they are put forward so
indirectly. Stronger evidence there could hardly be
to the strictly historical character of the narrative
than the peculiar and consistent reticence which is
observed on this head ; first one and then another
of those who are healed from various maladies being
expressly forbidden to proclaim their Healer, and
the crowds avoided which would have taken Him by
force to make Him King ; and yet all the time un-
mistakeable if not explicit hints thrown out. He is
greater than Jonah, greater than Solomon ; He alone
knows the Father ; none but the Father knows the
Son ; He alone gives rest and peace ; the yoke
which the disciples bear is His yoke ; He is the
great Judge who is to separate between the sheep
and the goats ; in that day the good deeds which
have been done to the poor are as if they had
been done to Him ; on the other hand, His claim
takes precedence of that even of the poor ; so exalted is His claim that to receive one of His
disciples is to receive Him, and to receive Him
is to receive the Father. Nowhere is the truth
to which St. Peter confessed distinctly expressed,
though everywhere it is implied, *Thou art the Christ,
the Son of the living God ;* and then at last
comes that warm and emphatic ratification, *Blessed
art thou, Simon Bar-jonah, for flesh and blood hath*

not revealed it to thee, but my Father which is in heaven.

This is our first ground. That which Jesus claimed for Himself cannot be wrong. We say with the centurion, as we look back over the history, *Truly this was the Son of God.*

(2) And then next there comes the strong consensus of the Apostolic age. In all ranks and schools and parties among Christians it is agreed that Christ died for our sins and rose again and sat down on the right hand of God. This is not the doctrine of St. Paul alone or of Apollos, but of St. Peter and St. Jude and St. John—we may add of St. James and of the nameless author of the work which is known as the Epistle to the Hebrews as well. Nothing can be more emphatic than the testimony which is borne by all but one of these writers. [The only exception is St. James, who has not occasion to bring out this particular doctrine, though we cannot doubt that he held it, for he names the Father and the Son together, and calls himself a servant of the Lord Jesus Christ [1]; and we know also that Christ appeared to him [2].] *The image of the invisible God, in whom it pleased the Father that all the fulness* (of the divine attributes) *should dwell,* writes St. Paul. *The brightness of His glory, and the express image of His substance,* writes the author of the Epistle to the

---

[1] St. James i. 1.   [2] 1 Cor. xv. 7.

Hebrews. *In the beginning was the Word, and the Word was with God, and the Word was God,* writes St. John. And there are a hundred other passages if we needed them. On other points there were controversies among Christians,—whether converts were to be circumcised or not ; whether prophecy was greater, or speaking with tongues ; whether it was right to be ascetic and to avoid certain kinds of meat ; what was the part played by angels in the work of creation and redemption ; when was to be the Second Coming, and what were its signs ; how Christians ought to behave in view of its near approach. All these were points that were really disputed. But there was no dispute that Christ was Lord, no dispute that He had risen, no dispute that He, and none but He, should judge the quick and the dead.

This is our second ground, the overpowering weight of consent in all quarters of the Christian world, of which we have abundant evidence little more than twenty years after the Ascension—the consent not of weaklings but of men of such strength of intellect and character as St. Paul and St. John.

(3) Then, lastly, we have the confirmation of this primitive belief by the deliberate verdict, long pondered and decisively given, of the later Church. Another hypothesis was tried on a large scale in the fourth and fifth centuries and found wanting. It was tried with all the advantages of imperial support,

with all the weight behind it of young and vigorous and warlike peoples. And yet not only was it solemnly and repeatedly condemned in the assemblies of Christendom, but the peoples who adopted it, one by one, gave it up until it vanished from the face of the earth. The verdict of history seems final against Arianism. Its champions were beaten in argument ; they were beaten in the field ; they were beaten in the hold which their tenets had upon the affections of their followers. It could not be said that Arianism had not a fair trial ; it had more than a fair trial ; but the result was a defeat so crushing as to leave no hope that it would ever successfully raise its head again.

We may however look beyond the horizon of Arianism, and we may say that the experience of more than eighteen centuries affords the very strongest presumption that nothing short of the Catholic doctrine will ever permanently satisfy the wants of Christian women and Christian men.

On these grounds we hold fast to the belief of the Church that *Our Lord Jesus Christ the Son of God is God and Man ; God of the Substance of the Father, begotten before the worlds ; and Man of the Substance of His Mother, born in the world ; perfect God, and perfect Man : of a reasonable soul and human flesh subsisting ; equal to the Father, as touching His Godhead, and inferior to the Father, as touching His Man-*

hood. Such is the clearly formulated Creed, which we hold with the whole Christian Church dispersed throughout the world. What then is the bearing of that Creed upon those passages in the Gospels in which He who is *perfect God and perfect Man* refers by name to the currently received authors of books of the Old Testament? Does it stamp and stereotype those names upon them absolutely and for ever?

Here will be apparent the reason why I think that it is a far sounder method not to ask this question until we know first what is the truth about the books in question, whether they were really the works of their reputed authors or not. It is not beyond the power of scholarly enquiry to determine this. Some think that it is determined already. I will not go so far as this, though I may have an opinion myself on which side the truth lies. Such an opinion, I admit, is different from certainty. It is different from the deliberate, sustained and tested assent of competent judges. That assent has not yet been obtained to such an extent as to pass from the region of the subjective to that of the objective, from opinion to ascertained fact.

We can, therefore, at present only speak provisionally and hypothetically. If it should be proved that the Law, as we have it, was not written by Moses, or that the 110th Psalm was not written by David, what

in that case should we say to the affirmations of the
Athanasian Creed? The question I think, for the
reasons I have given, is premature: but if we are
forced to answer it, thus much at least seems obvious,
that the explanation must lie in the fact that He of
whom we are speaking is not only God but Man.
The error of statement would belong in some way to
the Humanity and not to the Divinity. But here some
theologians tell us that no such mistake is possible
even to the Humanity. When they are confronted
with our Lord's own assertion that there was one
thing which He did not know—the hour of His own
Second Coming, they argue that the two things are
different, that imperfect knowledge is one thing,
erroneous teaching (though it is hardly teaching—
only a presupposition in what is taught) is another.
Again, when such an expression as *He maketh His
sun to rise* is referred in like manner to imperfect
science, that they admit, but maintain that questions
relating to the authorship of the Old Testament
touch more nearly the subject-matter of Revelation.
Are these distinctions valid? Are they valid enough
to be insisted upon so strongly as they must be if the
arguments based upon them are to hold good? I
greatly doubt it. They belong to a class of reasoning upon which I confess that I always look with
suspicion. They are *a priori* in their character: they
are not a definition of what *is*, but a laying down of

what *must* be : and that in a matter as to which I
question whether we are competent judges. The mere
phrase 'God-Man' is to me enough to make us
silent; it is enough at least to make our words be
'wary and few.' How shall we touch that mystery
just at its tenderest part, and speak of it as we might
speak of that which is well within our ken? To me
it seems that our wisdom is to abstain from theorizing
altogether until we are better assured as to the facts
about which we have to theorize.

One hypothesis, however, I think we may reject
beforehand. I should be loth to believe that our
Lord *accommodated* His language to current notions,
knowing them to be false. I prefer to think, as it has
been happily worded, that He '*condescended* not to
know[1].' It is part of that process of *kenosis* or ex-
inanition described at least in two places of St. Paul's
Epistles : *Though He was rich, yet for our sakes He
became poor*[2], and *Though He was in the form of God,
and counted it not a thing to grasp at that He should
be on an equality with God, He nevertheless emptied
Himself, taking the form of a servant*[3]. Though rich
in knowledge, He divested Himself at least of such
parts of that knowledge as enabled Him to take a real
humanity on the same footing with that of His fellow-
men. *He was made*, as the text has it, adopting the

---

[1] The phrase is Dr. Gregory Smith's in a letter to the *Guardian.*
[2] 2 Cor. viii. 9. [3] Phil. ii. 6, 7.

words of the Psalm, *a little lower than the angels.*
Some humiliation, some circumscription, His Advent
upon earth did involve. Before the fact I do not
think that we can say precisely how much humiliation
or circumscription. To do so is to take upon us too
much 'the mystery of things.'

Man is a curious being ; and he has many legitimate
objects for his curiosity. I doubt if this is one.
The data are too precarious ; they involve too great a
leap of the mind into the unknown. In regard to
these questions, I think we shall do better to ponder
the words of the Psalm : *Lord, I am not high-minded :
I have no proud looks. I do not exercise myself in
great matters, which are too high for me. But I
refrain my soul and keep it low, like as a child that is
weaned from his mother : yea, my soul is even as a
weaned child.*

That infinite ocean on the shores of which we play
may invite us to enter its fringe, but our footing is
soon lost as the bottom shelves away into depths
that for us are unfathomable. It is far better for us to
retire and do our allotted tasks upon the margin with
an outlook that sobers but does not affright us,
and with a heart not lifted up but chastened and
solemnized.

IX.

(St. Mary's, Oct. 19, 1890.)

PSALM cxix. 18.

*Open Thou mine eyes, that I may behold wondrous things
out of Thy Law.*

IN Christianity as a formulated system there are three main elements : (1) the common foundation of Hebrew religion as contained in the Old and New Testaments, but primarily in the Old; (2) a specially Christian element which is due to the life and work of Christ; (3) certain peculiar forms of expression, gradually determined upon after six centuries of keen controversy, which are to a large extent of Greek origin. Compared with these, the part really contributed by modern times is very small indeed. I do not say that modern thought is not very largely affecting our conception of Christianity; but so far it has done so only in a vague and indefinite way. The influence derived from this source has not succeeded in impressing itself upon Creeds and Articles. The really formative elements in these

I

will, I think, be found to be those which I have just enumerated.

At the present moment attention is being turned in full stream upon the first. It is likely also, if I am not mistaken, to be directed shortly to the third. The question of the Old Testament comes home to so many that it may be described as a popular question. The question of Greek thought can hardly reach these dimensions, but it cannot fail to attract to itself the careful study of thinking and far-seeing men. It is fraught with issues of considerable importance, which will perhaps occasion some anxiety at first, but which, I believe, will be found to bode good and not harm in the end.

I am led to make these remarks by the approaching publication of Dr. Hatch's Hibbert Lectures, in which, with the boldness and originality characteristic of him, he grappled with this problem, so far as my knowledge extends, for the first time on English ground. I do not doubt that these Lectures will be found greatly stimulating to thought, though another series of enquiries may be necessary in order to complete them. What Dr. Hatch has done has been to trace broadly the transition or transplantation of certain ideas and usages from the sphere of Hellenism to that of Christianity. What remains to be done is to apply a close analysis, one by one, to the works of the early Christian writers, so as to ascertain in what proportions the different elements of which we have spoken, and particularly the Greek element, were present in them.

A beginning has been made already in this direction in Germany, but not, I think, at all in England. It may perhaps be instructive to take a brief survey of the history of the subject and of the place at which the problem now stands. To Dr. Hatch, I rather think, the problem presented itself mainly as an abstract one. He had studied Philo and the Neo-platonists; he had studied the Stoics; and he observed in the Christian writers and in Christian controversies the recurrence of terms and conceptions which he had met with outside Christianity. To the Germans the problem came as in the first instance historical. It goes back, I suppose, to Baur. He definitely asked himself the question, How are we to account for that conception of Christianity which we find in possession of the field at the end of the second century, and increasingly so as time went on? Any one who looks at once with candour and with penetration at the Christianity of Irenæus at one end of the Christian world, and of Clement of Alexandria at the other, will see that there is a considerable interval between it and the Christianity of Christ and the Apostles. How was this interval to be accounted for? What shifting of elements had taken place? What was there in the one which there was not in the other? Baur, with his keen insight into the turning-points of history, took hold of this question and set himself to solve it. The solution which he proposed is well known. It proceeded on the lines of a ˙Hegelian antinomy: and it was to the effect that in the Apostolic age there were two great opposing forces, Jewish Christianity or Ebionism on the one hand and Pauline or Gentile Christianity on the other; by degrees these two opposites became reconciled by dropping their distinctive features, and Catholicism or the average creed of the Christian world at the year 200 was the result. Since the time of Baur a number of attempts have been made to improve upon his view. In the most successful of these attempts two negative factors were recognised and one positive. The negative factors were that the writers who immediately succeeded the Apostles failed really to grasp the deeper side of the teaching of St. Paul and that they also failed to understand the Old Testament [1]. The positive factor was that they imported into Christian speculation the principles which they had learned in the schools of Greek philosophy. The insight into the weakened apprehension of St. Paul's teaching has been rather widely shared. It is found in writers like Neander, who made the great mistake of supposing that this defective apprehension was caused by a return to

[1] On this point see the extracts in Appendix II.

Judaism. It was not a peculiarity of the Judaizing side of the Church, but was common in greater or less degree to all parties. The bringing out of the significance of the Old Testament was due to the strongest of all the disciples of Baur, who went back upon and corrected the conclusions of his master, in a work which has done more than any other with which I am acquainted to lay the foundations of a really sound conception of the course of events in the second century—Albrecht Ritschl. Since Ritschl published, in 1857, the second improved and developed edition of his work on the *Origin of the Old Catholic Church*, an excellent monograph, constructed upon his lines, came out in 1878 on the Christianity of Justin Martyr by Dr. Moritz von Engelhardt. Von Engelhardt was Professor at Dorpat, where I believe that he had for pupil Adolph Harnack, and I suspect that that fertile and able writer owes not a few of his best and soundest ideas to his old teacher. Quite recently a similar monograph by Werner on the Paulinism of Irenæus has appeared under his auspices, which is, however, not perhaps free from exaggeration. By all these writers alike the element which took the place of the missing constituents of Apostolic Christianity is sought in the current Greek philosophies, either apprehended immediately or filtering downwards into popular thought. We might sum up their construction of the history of doctrine very briefly thus. Through defective understanding first of St. Paul and then of the Old Testament, and through the influence of Greek ideas, there arose the older Catholicism of the early Christian centuries which has had a continuous development down to modern times. St. Augustine (partially) and the Reformers (again partially) rediscovered St. Paul; and I will make bold to add that the full rediscovering and full appropriating of the Old Testament are the special problem of our own day.

Many will think no doubt that this is an arrogant claim. I hope it is not made in any spirit of arrogance, but simply in deference to what seem to be the actual facts. I am anxious not to go a step beyond these. Of course it is true that a large and substantial part of the spirit of Christianity was perpetuated by Irenæus and his contemporaries. In particular one primary doctrine—the doctrine of the Logos, which fell in with the prevalent tendencies of thought, was seized hold of by them with great tenacity, and developed in great wealth and fulness of detail. But when we turn to another side of the New Testament Scriptures—to St. Paul's deep and inward conception of Faith, to the mingled attraction and awe with which he looked on the 'scandal of the Cross,' to that long series of oppositions between works and grace, law and promise, law and Gospel— in place of which we find Christianity regarded as itself merely a second revised system of law—we feel how much has been lost in the process of transmission. Even if we take a great fundamental idea like that of the Kingdom of God, which dominates alike the Old Testament and the New, we have to wait until we come to St. Augustine before it is worked out at all on an adequate scale; and even then it is not worked out exactly on the lines of the original conception. When we think of these things and of many more—the growth of the Messianic Idea, sublime personifications like the Servant of Jehovah, the use which Jeremiah makes of his doctrine of the twofold Covenant, all those wonderfully tender personal relations between God and His people implied in the Psalms and the Prophets which shrink into the cold ὄντως ὄν of the philosophers—when we think of all this, we cannot help being conscious that we do indeed see them more in their true proportions than the early Fathers did.

And yet let us be just to these founders of the Church and of Christian Theology to whom our debt is so large. Let us try to put in its right light the relation in which we stand to them. We think that we understand the Bible better than they did. There can be little doubt that we really do understand it better. But that is not because we are great men and they are small, but because the *Bible* is great and it has taken many centuries hitherto and will take a considerable time longer still before we understand it thoroughly. If the Jews so misinterpreted their own Bible as they certainly did in the time of our Lord, can we wonder if those who were not Jews by birth but brought up under very different conditions failed to understand it? I will not deny absolutely the truth that there is in allegory; but few of us would be willing to apply it as the universal key to the unlocking of the Old Testament, as some of the best and greatest minds of antiquity were ready to apply it. The fashioning of the methods by which the secret of the Old Testament is to be approached and elicited has taken many centuries. We are not yet agreed about it ; but I do not think that it is being too sanguine to feel that we are drawing nearer to it. We are beginning to feel the warmth and the life and the reality come back to those pale and shadowy figures. Isaiah and Hosea and Jeremiah no longer walk in a *limbus Patrum*, but we see them as they were among the forces by which they were actually surrounded. We see what they were as men ; we see what they were as exponents of a message from God ; we see the grand and glorious ideas which stirred within them in all their richness and fulness, conditioned, yet not wholly conditioned, by the world of thought and action in which they moved. We see these ideas linking themselves together, stretching hands as it were across the ages, the root-principles of the Old Testament running on into the New, and there attaining developments which may have been present to the Divine Mind—though they cannot have been present to the human instruments whose words went and came at its prompting. The famous saying of St. Augustine had a deeper sense than even he imagined for it. The New Testament was latent in the Old, not merely in the sense in which the type might be said to embrace the thing typified ; the Old Testament is patent in the New, not merely in the sense in which one series of events may be said to reflect another, but by a more vital and organic connexion. The further enquiry goes, the more impressively does it appear how much the lead- ing ideas of the New Testament had their way prepared for them, and by what strict continuity of growth they spring out of the leading ideas of the Old. There is a field here which I cannot help thinking will be ploughed and worked in the near future more effectively than it has been. But this idea of the organic connexion of thought with thought is com- paratively a recent one ; and to expect it to determine the work of the older commentators as it ought to determine ours would be as absurd as to expect that primeval man should be equipped with the encyclo- paedia of science.

But if there is such a valid excuse for the great

men of old as *Exegetes*, they hardly need an excuse at all in their other capacity as *Dogmatists*. If they are only judged fairly as they ought to be judged, that is with reference to their own time and circumstances, we shall be so far from scoffing at them that we shall be rather lost in wonder at the edifice which they reared. Certainly as much brain power went to the building up of this as to any of the best of our modern systems. Note the closeness and precision of thought ; note the accuracy with which one detail is fitted into another; note the multitude of speculations, sometimes, it is true, resting upon mistaken premises, but often really profound and striking, by which they are surrounded ; note the symmetry and harmony of the total result as it is summed up for instance in the Athanasian Creed— and any one who is capable of appreciating an intellectual construction, and can divest himself of his modern notions, will I think be most powerfully affected by it. One would like as an experiment to set down some well-trained modern scholar, with no appliances but his own unaided thinking, before the problems with which the ancients wrestled, and then to compare the result, say with a page of St. Cyril of Alexandria, and I do not think that we should find the comparison very flattering to our vanity. To say that the ancients worked with the tools which lay to their hands, that they operated with ideas which were the staple of the schools and lecture-rooms about them, is so much a matter of course that but for the extent to which it has been forgotten, it would hardly need to be insisted on. With our modern machinery we can produce circles and angles more exact than many an old-world craftsman, without possessing a tenth part of his skill of hand and eye.

And yet, on the other hand, I should be quite prepared to lay stress upon the fact that the formularies which were the product of all this intellectual subtlety and vigour have a value which is primarily historical and relative. They stand in living relation to the past rather than to the present. The problems of to-day have drifted away from them ; and if we go to them for a solution of these problems the answer we shall get must needs be imperfect and partial. May we not say that the simile which would best describe them would be that of the stations along our old coach-roads from which the traffic has been turned into other channels? They stand as landmarks which are speaking witnesses to a bygone time, but which no longer serve for the practical uses of the present, or which serve them so far only as the present is a direct outcome of the past. A great mass of wisdom is embodied in them—the wisdom not of an individual working in his study or his cell, but the wisdom of a Church or family of Churches all bringing their contributions to the common stock, and

testing each clause by the fire of an active and searching criticism. Given the premisses, and I think we
may say still that a better result could not have been
obtained; and that result has been verified by the
assumption and practice of ages. To this day I doubt
if any different conclusion could justify itself, approached along the same lines. So far as our problems
are identical I doubt if we shall have any need, or,
if we had the need, I doubt if we should have the
power, to reopen the decisions of united Christendom.
But the problems which press upon us most urgently
are not identical: the premisses which we have to
assume in dealing with them are a different set of
premisses, and it seems to me wrong to invoke laws
to decide cases which when they were framed were
never or but imperfectly contemplated.

The practical moral which I would venture to draw
from the whole situation is this, that we should not
spend our time in the cheap and easy but demoral-
izing employment of undervaluing the wisdom of our
forefathers and congratulating ourselves upon our
own, but that we should rather face and grapple with
the positive tasks which lie before us. We say that
the ancients had a defective understanding of the
Old Testament and a defective understanding of
St. Paul. There are doubtless some who will need
to have this proved to them: for them let us prove
it. And, having proved it, let us go on to the next

step and see that we get an understanding of both
these prime constituents of Christianity which is *not*
defective. Supposing it to be made out that there
has been in the formulating of Christian doctrine a
certain encroachment of Hellenism, the true way to
redress the balance is—not to disparage Hellenism,
which surely had a work to do in the providence of
God as well as Hebraism, but to go back to the old
Hebraic foundations of our religion and lay them
again more deeply and more firmly—or rather see
how they have been laid by an Architect wiser and
mightier than we. To do this as it ought to be done
would alone be the work of any ordinary generation.
How from all sides does the call come to us to be up
and doing! To us indolent dwellers in Zion who
have taken our ease by our rivers that flow softly,
thinking to enjoy our cakes of fine meal and our
wine, though we have left it to others to cut the corn
and to gather in the vintage and to bear all the
burden and heat of the day. I speak not to those
whose study is Theology alone. The *universitas
literarum* includes all the sciences: they form a
single body; and if one member suffers, all the others
suffer with it. Let us march altogether; let us take
our exercise altogether in the same *palaestra*—not
in dilettante fashion like half-hearted competitors,
but like men who are determined to run for the
prize and who are prepared to undergo the requisite

training before they enter for it. Then let the scholar help the theologian and the theologian the scholar; and let the historian lend a hand to and receive a hand from both. Sometimes it is said that the subjects of study are being exhausted. And perhaps it may be so with some subjects; but the date when anything of the kind will be true is far distant in ours. I have said enough to show what fruitful openings lie close to us. And the special beauty of theological study is that knowledge does not lie wide apart from practice, but that in proportion as we acquire the one we ought to be building up a body of principles to apply to the other. When we go for these to the Bible we are in no danger of being disappointed. And we shall find, or I am much mistaken, that each fresh discovery gilds with some new light or invests with some new reality, truths which had seemed to be trite and hackneyed. I do not say that every discovery will be what is called, on a superficial view, a 'confirmation.' It may be of that sort which sends us back and back again for further enquiry. But the ultimate result must be *to strengthen the stakes and lengthen the cords*, to deepen our apprehension and to extend its application. It is no less true now than ever it has been that the surest means of religious advance is to be sought in renewed study of the Bible. What we need especially at this moment is *freshness*, a real getting at the heart of the matter instead of dallying with the outside. And I question if we shall get this in any better way than by approaching our task under the guidance of Criticism and History—of Criticism and History not, as too often, dissevered from, but united with, Religion [1].

---

[1] It would be an important branch of the enquiry sketched above to determine precisely how far Greek thought enters into and is consecrated in the New Testament itself. The discussion would turn mainly round two points which cannot be regarded as settled, the origin of the Logos-doctrine in St. John and the theological affinities of the Epistle to the Hebrews. The purely Palestinian element in both may be larger than is sometimes supposed. Still it is probably true at the same time that Palestinian thought was putting out feelers in the direction of Hellenism. And I do not think it will be denied that the subsequent developments of the Logos-doctrine were developments in a straight line.

I BELIEVE it is literally true to say that Dr. Hatch was the first to raise the question discussed in his *Hibbert Lectures* 'on English ground'; but I ought not to have overlooked a course of lectures delivered about the same time (March 1888) at Princeton, U.S.A., by Dr. G. T. Purves, and published under the title *The Testimony of Justin Martyr to Early Christianity* (New York, Randolph). This is an independent counterpart to Von Engelhardt's work mentioned above, and is satisfactorily done.

APPENDIX I.

ON THE DATE OF THE PSALTER.

WHILE I am anxious not to step outside my proper pro-
vince by offering opinions upon a subject on which I am
conscious of possessing very partial knowledge, there is just
one of the problems of Old Testament criticism in regard
to which I should like to set down a few points which have
occurred to me, and submit them to the consideration of
more competent judges. The problem to which I refer is
one which is exciting a good deal of interest at the present
time, viz. the date of the Psalter. I approach it from the
side of the history of the formation of the O. T. Canon,
and the history of the Text and of certain accessories with
which this is intimately connected.

(1) The well-known passage in the prologue to Ecclesi-
asticus must no doubt be used with much caution. The
latest date that we can possibly assign to this is a little
after the year 132 B. C. This is assuming that the 38th
year mentioned in it is that of Euergetes II—a view to
which I think that I incline myself, though not with complete
confidence. If that were so, we must allow some further
interval (συγχρονίσας) for the actual composition of the prologue. But as evidence it would still go back some way
before rather than after 132 B. C., for the frequency with
which the writer repeats his phrase, in so short a compass
(*'by the law and the prophets, and by others that have followed*

K

their steps,' 'the reading of the law and the prophets and other books of our fathers,' 'the law itself and the prophets and the rest of the books'), seems to show that it was no novelty picked up by him in Egypt, but part of the mental stock which he brought with him. And I should greatly hesitate to adopt Dr. Edersheim's view (*Speaker's Comm. on Apocr.* ii. 5), that the writer himself gave rise to this tripartite division. He seems to me to refer to it in a way which would assume that it was already established.

In any case his language appears to imply a rather advanced stage in the history of the O. T. Canon. The conception of such a Canon is distinctly formed: certain books are set aside and marked off from the rest of literature: two of the three groups into which they are divided appear to be already defined, and the third is in process of definition. The stage arrived at is so distinctly that of collecting and arranging older materials that it is difficult to think of writings newly composed, as at once placed upon the same level with them. We must remember, also, that the writer of the prologue was not himself an Egyptian Jew; but *came to* Egypt—we may presume from Palestine or even from Jerusalem, the home of his grandfather (Ecclus. l. 27); so that the view represented would be that of the stricter Palestinian Jews, and it was within this stricter circle that the Psalter received its present circumscription. Although, therefore, the 'Wisdom of the Son of Sirach' was itself admitted into the Alexandrian Bible, we must not press this fact too far. Neither must we treat a book like the Psalter as if it were necessarily already closed. There is a laxity of outline around *the other books* which there is not in *the law and the prophets.* The Psalms of Solomon show us that psalms were still being written; and that at a much later date than this they could still gain admission into the larger Bibles. For instance, they were originally included in the collection of Cod. Alexandrinus, and still stand in the list of contents of that MS. On the whole, though I should not contend, on this ground at least, for the complete closing of the Psalter by the year 132 B.C., I should confess to an uneasy feeling if I admitted into it a Psalm headed *a Psalm of David*, but not really composed till the time of Hyrcanus.

(2) The next point has reference to the 'Psalms of Solomon' just mentioned. Does not a collection which goes by this name imply the existence, in a well-defined and substantive shape, of a previous collection of 'Psalms of David'? The Psalms of Solomon cover the years 63–48 B.C., and must have been composed or finished not long after the latter date. It would, however, of course, be too much to suppose that the title which they now bear was attached to them at once. Still, it cannot have been very long in coming. By the middle of the third century the collection has been augmented by five 'Odes of Solomon,' which, as the Psalms appear to have been reckoned at XVII, made up the total number to XXII, corresponding to the letters of the Hebrew alphabet[1]. The fondness of Jews and Hellenists for literary artifices of this kind is well known. Not only is the title thus firmly attached to them, but the collection has also a considerable history behind it (implying possibly translation, not only into Greek, but into Coptic, because the Psalms and Odes are both quoted in a Coptic work) by the year 250.

---

[1] The Gnostic treatise *Pistis Sophia*, dating from the middle of the third century, quotes the Second Ode as no. xix thus : *Tua vis luminis* ἐπροφήτευσεν *de his verbis per Salomonem in eius decima nona ode et dixit, Dominus super meum caput sicut corona,* etc. (ed. Petermann-Schwartze, p. 118 [76]).

(3) Some further light is thrown on the history of the Psalms as a collection by the New Testament. By the time that the Acts of the Apostles was written (if we may not say rather by the time of St. Paul's first missionary journey), not only is the collection complete, but it has received a fixed numbering. Ps. ii. 7 is quoted in Acts xiii. 33 expressly as *The Second Psalm*. And this quotation has an interesting history. There are traces of an extremely early reading known to Origen, and adopted by Hilary, by which *first* is substituted for *second*. And this variant numbering of the first two Psalms goes back beyond Origen to Justin, and beyond Hilary to Tertullian and Cyprian. Origen had seen the two Psalms combined in one of two Hebrew copies to which he had had access [1]. It seems, therefore, that the variation began in the Hebrew before it was transferred to the Greek; and we should thus have four distinct stages (the original Hebrew collection and numbering, the Hebrew variant, the Greek translation, and the Greek variant), all to be got through before the time of Justin; if the reading πρώτῳ were original, we should have to say before the time of St. Luke, or even of St. Paul. As a matter of fact, the reading is adopted by Lachmann, Tischendorf, and Tregelles; but it is not endorsed by Westcott and Hort, and being so clearly what is technically called a ' Western ' reading, cannot be pressed [2].

We cannot here be sure that we have an original wrong reading, implying a fourfold process of corruption, actually

[1] See Westcott and Hort, *ad loc.*

[2] I see that Dr. Cheyne connects the uniting of Pss. i. ii. with the reckoning of the whole number as 147, 'according to the number of the years of Jacob ' (*The Book of Psalms*, p. xiv). It is certainly surprising to find such an advanced stage of reflexion in the second century.

in New Testament times. But there are other examples
in the New Testament itself better attested and not less
significant. I will quote a few which have come to my
hands after no very long search: there are probably others
quite as important.

Rom. xv. 11 Καὶ πάλιν· Αἰνεῖτε πάντα τὰ ἔθνη τὸν Κύριον, καὶ
ἐπαινεσάτωσαν αὐτὸν πάντες οἱ λαοί.

> ἐπαινεσάτωσαν ΝΑΒCDE ; Chrys. *cod.* Jo.-Damasc.; *Edd.*
> ἐπαινέσατε FGLP *al. pler.*; Chrys. *codd.* Theodrt. *al.*

Ps. cxvi (cxvii). 1 Αἰνεῖτε τὸν Κύριον, πάντα τὰ ἔθνη, αἰνεσάτωσαν
αὐτὸν πάντες οἱ λαοί.

> αἰνεσάτωσαν Ν (*def.* B).
> ἐπεναινεσάτωσαν A (*sic*).
> ἐπαινέσατε RT (= ἐπαινέσαται Νᶜᵃ).

Here the right reading in Romans is undoubtedly ἐπαινεσάτωσαν. It is not so clear that the same word is right in
the Psalm: the simple form αἰνεσάτωσαν would compete
with it, if not also ἐπαινέσατε. The text of the Epistle is
thrown decidedly into the scale of A, and stands or falls
with it.

Rom. iii. 4 Καθὼς γέγραπται· "Οπως ἂν δικαιωθῇς ἐν τοῖς λόγοις
σου καὶ νικήσεις ἐν τῷ κρίνεσθαί σε.

> νικήσεις ΝΑDE, *minusc. aliq.*; La². Ti. Tr³. WH.
> νικήσῃς BGKL, *al. pler.*; La¹. Tr¹.

Ps. l (li). 6 "Οπως ἂν δικαιωθῇς ἐν τοῖς λόγοις σου καὶ νικήσῃς
ἐν τῷ κρίνεσθαί σε.

> νικήσῃς ΝBRT (*ex sil.* Swete ; *def.* A).
> νικήσεις *minusc. aliq. ap. Holmes.*

Here νικήσεις is probably right in Romans (B has a weak
place in the Epistles at which the alternative reading seems
to come in), and νικήσῃς in the Psalm.

Eph. iv. 8 Διὸ λέγει· 'Αναβὰς εἰς ὕψος ᾐχμαλώτευσεν αἰχμαλω-
σίαν καὶ ἔδωκεν δόματα τοῖς ἀνθρώποις.

ᾐχμαλώτευσεν ℵBCDEFGKP etc.; Edd.
ᾐχμαλώτευσας AL, minusc. aliq. al.
ins. καὶ ℵ°BC*D°KLP al. pler.; Tr. WH¹.
om. καὶ ℵ*AC²D*FG cl.; La. Ti. WH².
ἐν ἀνθρώποις F°ʳG, patr. aliq.

Ps. lxvii (lxviii). 19 ἀναβὰς εἰς ὕψος ᾐχμαλώτευσας αἰχμαλω-
σίαν, ἔλαβες δόματα ἐν ἀνθρώπῳ.

ἀναβὰς B*R*.
ἀνέβης ℵ°ᵃBᵃᵇRᵃ.
ἀνέβη ℵ* (def. A), Lat.-Vet.
ᾐχμαλώτευσας ℵ°ᵃBR.
ᾐχμαλώτευσεν ℵ*, Lat.-Vet.
ἀνθρώπῳ B* ᵒᵇ ᵇ.
ἀνθρώποις ℵBᵃRᵃ.

Here the true reading is undoubtedly ἀναβὰς ᾐχμαλώτευσεν
in Ephesians, and probably ἀναβὰς ᾐχμαλώτευσας in the
Psalm, though ἀνέβη ἀνέβης and ᾐχμαλώτευσεν are all early
readings.

There is then, perhaps, some doubt as to the first of these
passages: the New Testament reading may, perhaps (though
not certainly), be right. In the other two passages it is
pretty certainly wrong. But the error is something more
than a mere isolated lapse: it involves in each case the
endorsement in the New Testament, not only of a wrong
reading, but of a wrong type of text: already in New
Testament times the leading texts of the LXX have begun
to diverge, and corrupt texts have gained currency. The
evidence so far has been confined to the Psalms; but the
same conclusion would hold good of the other books: e.g.
in Rom. xi. 34, and 1 Cor. ii. 16, two distinctively A-readings
(σύμβουλος αὐτοῦ and συμβιβάσει) are adopted from Isa. xl. 13.

The text in which these phenomena are found clearly is not a young one.

(4) The conclusion just arrived at is confirmed by reference to Philo. Of the readings quoted by Dr. Hatch (*Ess. in Bibl. Greek*, p. 173) the following may be taken.

Ps. xlv (xlvi). 5 τοῦ ποταμοῦ τὰ ὁρμήματα εὐφραίνουσι τὴν πόλιν τοῦ Θεοῦ.

τὸ ὅρμημα εὐφραίνει, one cursive, Lat.-Vet.: and so Philo.

Ps. xciii (xciv). 9 ὁ πλάσας ὀφθαλμούς, οὐ κατανοεῖ;

ὀφθαλμούς אB : and Philo.
τοὺς ὀφθαλμούς R.
τὸν ὀφθαλμόν A.
ὀφθαλμόν אᶜᵃ.

[The other variants of Philo's text in this passage are not to our purpose.]

Here it is, perhaps, probable that Philo is right, in which case this reading would be of no significance. The Hebrew, however, has the singular, and antecedently it would have seemed rather more likely that the plural would be substituted when the scribe no longer had the Hebrew before him, i.e. in some copy of the LXX after the first. But the decision must turn ultimately on the value of the combination אB, which is not as yet quite a fixed quantity. In the first passage Philo has against him אABRT: still there can be no doubt that his reading, though hardly right, is a very early one. We are again on the trace of a divergent family—represented by Lat.-Vet. Philo would thus testify to the existence of this family quite at the beginning of the first century.

(5) It were much to be wished that some competent scholar would set himself to work out systematically the

history of the *Titles to the Psalms*. An excellent beginning has
recently been made by Dr. Neubauer (*Studia Biblica*, ii. p. 1 ff.)
for the later history as it may be traced especially through the
Jewish interpreters. This alone is valuable; but we want a
searching examination of the earlier history—backwards, let
us say, from the Hexapla. We need to have more exactly
defined the stages which the titles have passed through up to
that date. Dr. Neubauer has brought out quite clearly that
the later Jewish commentators had no tradition on the
subject. Some of the best of them make shrewd guesses;
but their guesses are not different in kind from those
which are made in our own day. We go back to the
Targum, an Aramaic paraphrase, made probably by a Jew
who had some knowledge of Greek, in the fourth century,
and still we find the same thing. From the Targum we
turn to the Hexapla; and from that we find that even our
earliest authorities, the Greek Versions, are equally at fault.
Let us take one or two of the first that occur. I give a
literal rendering of the Greek in each case.

PSALM IV.

LXX. εἰς τὸ τέλος ἐν ψαλμοῖς ᾠδὴ τῷ Δαυείδ.

ἐν ψαλμοῖς ᾠδὴ אB.
ψαλμὸς ᾠδῆς R.
ψαλμὸς A.

'For the end; in psalms; a song of David:' i. e.,
as explained by Eusebius and Theodoret, 'a psalm
relating to things which are to happen at the end [of
the world].' It seems that the Hebrew taken in
this way might possibly = 'for performance' (Delitzsch,
ad loc. ed. 3).

AQUILA. τῷ νικοποιῷ ἐν ψαλμοῖς μελῴδημα τῷ Δαυείδ.

'For the victor; in psalms; a melody of David.'

Gregory of Nyssa combines the two renderings 'victory' and 'end:' εἰς τὸ τέλος ὅπερ ἐστιν ἡ νίκη. And Chrysostom remarks that in Hebrew the same word means 'end' and 'victory,'—a statement which appears to be really true of different periods in the language (Delitzsch).

SYMMACHUS. ἐπινίκιος διὰ ψαλτηρίων ᾠδὴ τῷ Δ.
'Of victory, on psalteries, a song of David.'

THEODOTION. εἰς τὸ νῖκος ἐν ὕμνοις ψαλμὸς τῷ Δ.
'For victory, in hymns, a psalm of David.'

R. V. (= Heb.) 'For the chief musician; on stringed instruments; a psalm of David.'

This appears to be the true meaning: the psalm is to be handed to the choirmaster for performance on stringed instruments.

PSALM VIII. [There are the same variants for the word meaning 'choirmaster.']

LXX. and SYMMACHUS. ὑπὲρ τῶν ληνῶν.
'For the wine-presses' (i. e. vintage).

AQUILA and THEODOTION. ὑπὲρ τῆς γεθθίτιδος.
'For the Gittite' (fem.).

TARGUM. 'On the harp which came from Gath.'

A. V. 'Upon Gittith' (i.e. a kind of harp).

R. V. 'Set to the Gittith' (i.e. a jubilant tune, 'March of the men of Gath,' Hitzig).

PSALM IX.
LXX. εἰς τὸ τέλος ὑπὲρ τῶν κρυφίων τοῦ υἱοῦ.
om. τοῦ υἱοῦ R.

'For the end concerning the secrets of the son.'
Pro occultis filii, Vulg.

AQUILA. τῷ νικοποιῷ νεανιότητος τοῦ υἱοῦ.
'For the victor of the youth of the son.'

SYMMACHUS. ἐπινίκιον περὶ τοῦ θανάτου τοῦ υἱοῦ.
'A victor's ode concerning the death of the son.'

THEODOTION and QUINTA. τῷ νικοποιῷ ὑπὲρ ἀκμῆς τοῦ υἱοῦ.
'For the victor on the coming of age of the son.'

SEXTA. εἰς τὸ τέλος νεανικότης τοῦ υἱοῦ.
'For the end, youth of the son.'

TARGUM. To praise, on the occasion of the death of the man who came out from the camp (Goliath).

R. V. 'For the chief musician; set to Muth-labben; a psalm of David.'

Of these, Aquila and Sexta are sheer nonsense, and Theodotion and Quinta little better. It is very doubtful whether anything can be made of LXX. There is, however, a consistent sense in Symmachus, whose rendering points to some such event as the death of Goliath (Targ., David ben Abraham, and others), Absalom, the son of Bathsheba, etc. No doubt the reference is really to a tune, the name of which R. V. discreetly veils.

These examples might be multiplied to any extent; but enough will have been given to show how helpless the Greek versions are from the earliest to the latest. There is clearly no tradition in the strict sense, but each of the translators makes the best conjecture that he can. It is important to observe that the second-century versions are no better off than the Septuagint. Otherwise we might have supposed that the knowledge of what the titles originally meant, though lost at Alexandria, had been preserved in Palestine. This appears to be the explanation suggested by Hupfeld (*Die Psalmen*, p. 46). Even so, we could hardly have accepted it without hesitation, because there was so much intercourse between the Jews of Egypt and those of Palestine as to make it difficult to believe that a whole section of knowledge could thus have been possessed by the one and not possessed by the other. We remember at once that, according to the Pseudo-Aristeas, the seventy translators themselves came from Palestine : we think at once of Onias, of the grandson of Jesus, the son of Sirach, of the letters at the opening of 2 Maccabees, of Agrippa I at Alexandria, and of the constant stream of Jewish immigrants into Egypt, and of pilgrims from Egypt to Jerusalem. If the Alexandrian Jews had forgotten what the titles meant, it would have been easy enough for them to get to know. But then we find that in the second century of our own era the Jews of Palestine were just as ignorant; and not only in the second century, but quite early in the century, in circles so well informed as that of Aquila, and with hardly a generation intervening since the fall of the Herodian temple. It is difficult to think of the break in the tradition on such a point as occurring between Hillel and Akiba.

On one point I have not ventured to touch, the possibility that some of the varieties of rendering might be explained by differences of reading in the Hebrew text. The Hebraists must tell us what opening there is for this. In any case there will be at least the following stages: (1) the Hebrew psalm composed; (2) a title attached to it— often a title which implies that the true circumstances of its composition are forgotten ; (3) then further the meaning of the title itself lapses from memory ; (4) the great current version is made into Greek with titles already misunderstood ; (5) a secondary group of versions arises under different geographical and historical conditions and in connexion with several distinct schools or parties, yet the same ignorance prevails in all. Not only are these distinct stages, but they must each be of considerable length. If we must allow for variants in the Hebrew, one of them would be still further prolonged.

I cannot attempt to put a definite estimate upon these data ; for that a more special knowledge is required. I would only venture to commend them to the attention of those who have that knowledge. At the same time I confess that, on a *prima facie* view, it appears to me that four out of the five stages mentioned above will have to be got through at the latest by the time of Hillel. But even Hillel was not the first of the Scribes: and, working back from him, we are soon brought to the age of the Maccabees. It seems to me that this age is the latest which can be assigned for the completion of the Psalter. I am strongly tempted to go further, and to add, that in spite of the indications which are often thought to point to Maccabean Psalms, the doubt is still present to my mind whether even this is not descending too low.

NOTE.

I HOPE that the object of this Appendix will not be misunderstood. It was intended to be wholly tentative. So far as it might seem to express opinion on the date of the Psalter, it was opinion not formed but forming. I imagine that there must be many others in the same state of mind as myself, feeling their way gradually on the subject, and resting for the moment in temporary hypotheses and half-way positions, prepared to go either forwards or backwards as the case may be, but wishing not to commit themselves to definite affirmations until they feel more sure of their ground. I took the opportunity of the issue of this volume to set down in print some of these tentative hypotheses, partly for my own sake, as a help in the process of thinking, and partly for the sake of others at a similar stage to myself, to whom they might render a like service. The points chosen for discussion of course cover only a small extent of ground; they were chosen not so much for their intrinsic importance as for certain links of connexion with my own more special studies. Any hypothesis to be finally accepted as true must needs embrace all parts of a question; and to break up that question into some of its smaller subdivisions may be a real step towards obtaining their solution.

To attempt more than this would have been presumption on my part ; and it would have been particularly ill-timed in view of the near publication of Dr. Cheyne's *Bampton Lectures.* I join most cordially in the interest with which those lectures are expected, and I promise myself much instruction from them. It will have appeared from the body of this work that it will be no serious or insuperable shock to me if some of the Psalms, more or fewer, should ultimately be referred to Maccabean times. In this, as in all else, we must be guided simply by the evidence. Still I seem to see difficulties in the way ; and I was not sorry to have an opportunity of stating some of these difficulties in a shape which I hope is free from controversy.

My purpose in doing so has been answered to an extent beyond what I could have anticipated through the kind permission which has been given me to print portions of a letter from Dr. Driver which form a running comment on the questions raised in the Appendix, especially the last on which I was most anxious to have his opinion. On this in particular I think it will be felt that great light is thrown; but apart from that a lesson may be learnt from the combined open-mindedness and caution which are characteristic of a scholar.   Dr. Driver writes as follows:—

' On (1) I have little to say. The passage is generally admitted to presuppose the threefold division of the Canon recognised by the Jews, though it could not be taken as *proving* that the third comprised all the books which it now contains. Certainly, some very late Psalms—though it is difficult to say positively *how* late—have David's name attached to them (ciii, cxxiv, cxxxiii, cxxxix, cxliv, cxlv,—late, from the language). The *distribution* of Davidic Psalms, especially in Books III-V, is difficult to understand; if cx. for instance be his, or date from his time, why does it stand where it does, in a late collection, and after two which are certainly much later than David's time (cviii. a composite Psalm = parts of lvii. and lx.)? One opinion is that there was a collection (or collections) gradually added to, the nucleus of which was ancient and was probably really Davidic; in this case the collection might be known as "David's," and a Psalm taken from it, though really much later, may have been inscribed " David's." This certainly seems to be the explanation of the Asaph-Psalms. That a Psalm composed in the second century should be inscribed "David's" is no doubt singular; but is it more so than that Psalms composed in the fifth or fourth century should be so inscribed? The Chronicler (1 Chron. xvi. 7 ff.) attributes to David a *composite* Psalm, composed of three post-exilic Psalms. Indeed, he consistently treats David as the founder of the Temple-services, as they were organized in his own day, representing in this, no doubt, the current opinion of his age (300 B.C.). Has not this something to do with the (incorrect) ascription of Psalms to David ? I own that I sympathize with your 'uneasy feeling'; but I am not sure whether, in order for it to be decisive, we ought not to be clearer than we are as to the precise motives and grounds on which Psalms were said to be "David's." '

I should be far from supposing that the argument of the Appendix was in any way 'decisive': but the observation as to the usage of the Chronicler seems to me important, and such as might well furnish a starting-point in the investigation of these Davidic collections. Is it not remarkable that of the three Psalms (cv, xcvi, cvi) which the Chronicler—whether for the first time or, as I should prefer to think, following some previous editor—combines together and ascribes to David only one (Ps. xcvi=xcv, LXX) has an extant title attributing it to David, and that not in the Hebrew but only in the LXX? It would be natural to suppose that there would be two stages in the history of these collections ; the first, if we may so call it, the fluid stage, during which the contents of scattered and fragmentary MSS. would be painfully brought together by scribes and editors; and the second, during which the collections so formed would be publicly known and circulated. In the first stage I can readily understand how—often perhaps from mere accidental juxtaposition—Psalms not really written by David might come to have his name attached to them. But in the second period it seems to me far less easy to realize to ourselves the process by which Psalms newly composed would get incorporated into existing and known collections. Is not the Chronicler's in fact a case in point? Should we not have expected that his influence alone would have been enough to bring the name of David into the titles of the three Psalms, if not to gain a place for the one composite Psalm in the Psalter? Yet this has not been done. The inference seems to be suggested—and I should have thought that it was in keeping with the part assigned by the Chronicler to David in connexion with the Temple-music generally—that the second period had already been reached, and that the Davidic collections would in the natural course of things be closing, if not closed. There is however another important point, to which my attention is also called by Dr. Driver, that with very few exceptions the Psalms ascribed to David are not liturgical or such as in the first instance would have been composed for use in public worship.

On the next point Dr. Driver briefly touches :—

'(2) No doubt "Davidic" collections existed prior to 63-48 B.C. The problem is, How did they arise ?'

My argument was (*valeat quantum*) that a Solomonic Psalter implied a previous Davidic Psalter; but I admit that the condition might be satisfied by the existence of smaller collections under the name of David without supposing that the larger collection went as a whole by his name. Any argument of this sort would be superfluous if these Davidic collections went back as far as the time of the Books of Chronicles. Professor Kirkpatrick, in his excellent edition just published of the *First Book of the Psalms*, p. xxxvii, gives a new and more important turn to the argument by pointing to the chasm in thought and tone which separates the Psalms of Solomon from the Canonical Psalms. He urges, after Schürer, that the righteousness of these later Psalms is already that of Pharisaic Judaism.

My remarks upon the bearing of the history of the text of the Greek Psalter on the age of that version, and therefore ultimately of the Hebrew original, were prompted by the belief that this was a train of reasoning which had proved of use in regard to the New Testament and had not yet been opened up in reference to the Old. Dr. Driver's comments are as follows :—

'(3) The point is an interesting one, and deserves further investigation. Is not a wider induction needed to show whether the variations are accidental (i.e. due to quotation from memory, &c.), or whether they tend to agree systematically with A (or any other MS. or group of MSS.)? Another point arises in connexion with the fact that A (as is well known), as compared with B, exhibits a text that has constantly been corrected so as to conform with the Hebrew (see e. g. 1 Sam. i. 1, and continually) : do the variants in the N. T. approximate also to the Heb.? And if so are they corrections which might have been made independently or will they have been borrowed from texts of the LXX?

Variations resulting from intentional correction would not presuppose such a long interval of time as those arising from the ordinary sources of textual corruption.'

I am glad that Dr. Driver encourages the prosecution of this line of inquiry. No doubt there are many possibilities which will have to be duly considered on the right hand and on the left. I do not think, however, that the two disturbing elements which he mentions are likely to prove of great importance. Variants in a quotation are seldom due to mere accident where they coincide with MS. readings of the original text. The chief point to be considered is whether these MS. readings derive their origin from the quotation and are not independent of it—a case which is more than usually possible with quotations from the O. T. in the N. T. There is no doubt frequently a reflex action from N. T. quotations upon the text of O. T. MSS. But the *prima facie* tendency of criticism will probably be to exaggerate the amount of corruption due to this cause. Many O. T. variants can be proved to have been in existence before it can well have come into operation. In such cases the other alternative must be chosen—that the N. T. writers were themselves making use of a divergent text. The other cause, assimilation to the Hebrew, is also one that can be allowed for without much difficulty. I have not specially tested the O. T. quotations in the N. T. text of A. The archetype at least of one very important line of N. T. text can be traced to a scribe who possessed a knowledge of Hebrew; but this is not the line of A. It should be remembered too that A is not so distinctly the representative of a particular line of text in the N. T. As a matter of fact the number of authorities for the early history of the text of the N. T. is so great that corruption from the Hebrew would soon reveal itself. The instances of readings given in the Appendix had undergone a certain amount of preliminary sifting; and I believe that they will be found to belong to varied types and by no means only to that of A.

Points (3) and (4) practically go together, and on the second of these Dr. Driver makes no separate remarks; but I had specially invited his opinion on (5), and on this I will give what he has been so good as to write to me in full.

'I doubt greatly whether much weight is to be attached to the ignorance of the LXX. The LXX, in all parts of their translation (which of course, as its varying character shows, is the work of very different hands, and in all probability was only completed gradually), are apt to stand aloof from the Palestinian tradition; they frequently show themselves to be unfamiliar not only with uncommon or exceptional words, but even with those which one would have expected to be well known. This may be illustrated, in particular, from the very word from which the Hebrew term rendered "precentor" is derived. The verb, נצח, of which מְנַצֵּחַ, "precentor," is the participle, is never found in the pre-exilic literature; it occurs only in the Chronicles and Ezra; i. e. it was employed in Palestine, by an author writing c. 300 B.C., and, it may reasonably be assumed, was understood there at the time. It is not mostly used with reference to music; it denotes properly *to be pre-eminent*[1], then more generally *to preside* or *superintend*, the sense *to lead* (in music) being merely a special application of this idea. It is hardly possible that a word familiarly known in Palestine, c. 300 B.C., and (in its musical connexion) retained in use in the Temple services, should have had its meaning forgotten there during the period of 1-2 centuries which may have elapsed between 300 B.C. and the date at which the LXX translation of the Chronicles and Ezra was made; yet the translators of these books have evidently no idea of its meaning when used in that connexion. The following is a synopsis of the passages in which the verb occurs :—

1 Ch. xv. 21 R.V. to lead, LXX τοῦ ἐνισχῦσαι[2].
  xxiii. 4 R.V. to oversee, LXX ἐργοδιῶκται.

---

[1] In Aramaic, *to be distinguished*, cf. Dan. 6, 3 [Aram. 4], often also *to prevail, triumph*; the substantive נִצְחָא, ܢܶܨܚܳܐ *victory*. This *Aramaic* usage explains some of the renderings of the term to be noticed below.

[2] For the association of the idea of *strength* with what is (in reality

2 Ch. ii. 2 [Heb. 1]¹ R.V. to oversee, LXX ἐπιστάται.

18 [Heb. 17]¹ R V ovеrsсeis, LXX ἐργοδιῶκται.

xxxiv. 12 R.V. to set forward, R.V. *marg.* to preside (over it), LXX ἐπισκοπεῖν.

13 R.V. set forward, LXX ἐπί.

Ezra iii. 8 R.V. to have the oversight, LXX omit (ἐπί representing the following עַל).

9 R.V. to have the oversight, LXX similarly omit.

In all these passages except the first the LXX render freely or make use of some general equivalent ; in 1 Chron. xv. 21, in spite of the reference being manifestly to music, they show themselves to be entirely unacquainted with the meaning of the verb. Their rendering, in the Psalms ², of the title לַמְנַצֵּחַ (which they must have vocalized, not as a *participle* לַמְנַצֵּחַ but as a *substantive* לְמִנְצָּח) by εἰς τὸ τέλος (*with* the article) is plainly to be accounted for by their rendering of the common לָנֶצַח "for ever" by εἰς τέλος (*without* the article) ; but in the light of what has been said, it cannot be held to show that the sense of the word was unknown at the time in *Palestine*; it only shows that it was unknown in *Alexandria*. The usage of the verb נִצַּח appears to me to constitute a presumption that the sense "precentor" for the participle מְנַצֵּחַ originated in *post*-exilic times; its use in Hab. iii. 19 is not opposed to this view ; for it may well have been added afterwards, at a time when the ode of Habakkuk was used in the services of the Temple³.

---

or appearance) the same root, see Is. xxv. 8, Jer. xv. 18, LXX. The LXX not unfrequently give to a *Hebrew* word a sense which the root only bears in Aramaic; and it is probable that they were led to this rendering of נצח by the sense *to prevail* which the root has in Aramaic.

¹ These two verses are plainly based upon 1 Ki. v. 14–15, with slight modifications—amongst others, with the substitution of the late word נצח, for רדה 'bear rule,' used in the book of Kings.

² In Hab. iii. 19, τοῦ νικῆσαι (i.e. לְמְנַצֵּחַ, vocalized as an *infin.*, and explained from the *Aramaic* : compare the preceding notes).

³ I do not, however, desire by this to be supposed to hold that the Temple-psalmody itself originated only after the exile. I have no doubt that the beginnings of this were much earlier; the 'Singers,' who returned in B.C. 536 (Ezra ii. 41), must have been the descendants of those who had discharged similar functions in the pre-exilic Temple. And some of the other technical terms, as *Shiggaion*, *the Gittith*, &c., may also well be of ancient origin; but they hardly prove anything as to the

But whether this be the case or not, 1 Chron. xv. 21 is evidence that the word was understood in Palestine c. 300 B.C.[1] : either, therefore, it gradually fell out of use, and its meaning thus gradually became obscured in the centuries following ; or (as this seems hardly probable during the continuance of the Temple-services) the break in the tradition must have taken place in the great dispersion which overtook the nation after the destruction of Jerusalem by Titus, A.D. 70. In either case the revisers of the Greek translation of the O.T., who lived in the next century, Aquila, Symmachus, and Theodotion, will have sought to recover the lost meaning of the technical terms of Hebrew music, by etymological combinations, in which they were much influenced by their knowledge of the Aramaic dominant at the time. Hence their rendering of מנצח by νικοποιὸς or ἐπινίκιον.

'In the case of Aquila there is another point also to be borne in mind. Aquila was essentially an *innovator* : he was a pupil of R. Akiba, who introduced new and highly artificial methods of interpretation[2] : he made it his aim, even at the cost of the sense, to reproduce particles; in particular, he cultivated etymological renderings. Because פָּתַר means a *diadem*, he rendered in Ps. xxii. 13 the bulls of Bashan פָּתְּרִינִי by διεδηματίσαντό με ; because עֲרֻגָה signifies a *raised flower-bed* (Cant. v. 13), i.e. πρασιά, he rendered the verb עָרַג *to long* or *pant* in Joel i. 20 by ἐπρασιώθη ; the Hebrew word for *oil* he represented etymologically by στιλπνότης. The root נצח expressed to him the idea of *victory* (cf. the Aramaic usage referred to above[3]); hence he used νῖκος not only in Isa. xxv. 8 (where, even though incorrect, it would yield a suitable sense[4]), but even where it produces no sense at all, as Ps. lxxiv. 1 " Wherefore, O God, hast Thou cast us off *unto victory*?" (similarly in v. 10, and Ps. lxxix.

---

date of the Psalm to which they are attached ; for even after their true meaning had been forgotten, they might still have been employed conventionally to denote particular tunes, or kinds of melody, and attached as such to Psalms of late origin.

[1] The *style* of 1 Ch. xv. 1–24 (as of the other passages quoted, in which נצח occurs) shows that it was written by the Chronicler himself, and was not taken by him from earlier sources.

[2] For some account of R. Akiba's methods, see Dr. Pusey, ' *What is of faith as to everlasting punishment ?*' p. 79 ff.

[3] And see also 1 Sam. xv. 29, RV. *marg.*; Hab. i. 4, RV. *marg.* ; Lam. iii. 18, LXX; 1 Ch. xxix. 11, LXX and RV. (rightly).

[4] So also Theodotion, and in the quotation 1 Cor. xv. 54.

5 '). Aquila's renderings are essentially *artificial*[2]; they prove nothing as to either the presence or the absence of genuine traditional knowledge possessed by well-informed circles in his time.

'The origin of the Targum of Ps. ix. *title* is manifest. Goliath is called in 1 Sam. xvii. 4 "the man of the *bênaim*, or of the space *between* ("*bên*") the two armies (the μεταίχμιον)," i.e. the *champion*; here Hebrew words occur which might apparently mean "on the death of the *bên*." The similarity of *bên* in the title of Ps. ix to *bênaim* (which—looking at the *form* alone—might be its dual) in 1 Sam. xvii. 4 is quite sufficient ground for a Targumist to interpret the one passage by the other, and to understand the "*bên*" here as denoting Goliath. The phrase used in the Targum here, "On the death of the man who came forth *from between* the camps," is nearly the same as that in the Targum of 1 Sam. xvii. 4 " And there came forth a man *from between* them, from the camps of the Philistines." '

This goes far to cut away the ground from the argument I had used. It is clear that both in the LXX and Aquila tradition played a very subordinate part. The only point on which I have still a lingering doubt is whether the dispersion which overtook the nation after the destruction of Jerusalem by Titus in A.D. 70, is enough to constitute a real break in tradition where such has to be postulated. The Rabbinical schools soon found a rendezvous at Jamnia ; the succession of Rabbis goes on without interruption, and there must have been many priests dwelling in the country, like Zacharias (Luke i. 39), who escaped the general massacre. At a time when the Jews were so alive to the memories of their past, it is less easy to suppose a breach of continuity which might have been credible enough in an older generation.

---

[1] The same false rendering of נצח 'for ever' by 'unto victory' is found in some parts of the LXX : 2 Sam. ii. 26; Am. i. 11, viii. 7; Lam. v. 20 ; Job xxxvi. 7,—except in the last passage, to the entire ruination of the sense. Aquila's νεανιότητος in Ps. ix. *title* is a similar etymological rendering of על־מות, treated as one word עַלְמוּת.

[2] See this abundantly illustrated by Dr. Field, *Hexapla*, pp. xxi–iii.

APPENDIX II.

SOME EXTRACTS FROM RECENT CRITICISM ON THE DEFECTIVE APPREHENSION OF THE OLD TESTA-MENT IN THE EARLY CHURCH.

THE diversion of the stream of genuine Old Testament influence from the Early Church, during the formative period of its theology, is a fact of so much importance in itself, and one which is so little appreciated generally in England, that I will venture to give a few extracts from recent German writers bearing upon it. When we read the New Testament we see that, not only the Gospels, but the whole teaching of St. Paul, St. Peter, and St. John is in the most vital contact with the Old Testament. One of the greatest wonders of the New Testament is indeed the extent to which what we should call a strictly historical conception of the Older Dispensation is embodied in it, at a time when anything deserving of the name was so rare in the secular philosophers and historians. But when we turn to the second century, all is changed. Think of the references to Jewish history in the Epistles to the Galatians and Romans, and then (e. g.) in the Epistle of Barnabas; or observe the treatment of fundamental Pauline ideas in writers like Clement of Rome and Justin, and trace the defect in their teaching to its cause. This is the way in which the problem is worked out by Ritschl[1] :—

[1] I have not scrupled to use a slight amount of paraphrase, both in this and the following extracts, so as to make the German read more easily and naturally in English.

'Although Clement maintains in words the root-idea of the Apostle that the believer is redeemed from his sins, and that God has thus through Christ placed the believer in a specific relation to Himself, he has failed to understand the true significance of this thought, and grounds the relation of the believer to God on his attitude of repentance occasioned by the Death of Christ. The cause of this phenomenon is to be sought, not in the greater stress laid upon the moral attitude of the individual, which can only be regarded as a co-operating factor, but in the inability of a Gentile to master the Old Testament background of the leading features of the Apostle's teaching (die Unfähigkeit des Heiden, der richtigen alttestamentlichen Voraussetzungen der aposto-lischen Grundideen sich zu bemächtigen).' (*Entstehung d. altkathol. Kirche*, 2nd ed., Bonn, 1857, p. 282.)

Again, it is remarked of Justin, that while he connects re-demption with the Death of Christ, and does not omit to men-tion the condition of faith, ' this faith is not conceived of as faith *in Christ*; and instead of meaning with him that central function of the will which surrenders itself to the Person of Christ it is resolved into repentance and active obedience (Werkgehorsam), and the whole efficacy of the Death of Christ shrinks into the condition by which this state of things is realized (beschränkt die Wirkung des Opfers Christi auf die Be-dingung dieses empirischen Verhaltens).' Here, too, as in the case of Clement, Ritschl accounts for the confusion by saying that Justin as a Gentile-Christian had not ' that true under-standing of the Apostle's root-ideas which was to be derived from the Old Testament rightly interpreted ' (*ibid.* p. 304).

What Ritschl has thus said of particular writers and cer-tain particular doctrines, Overbeck takes up and applies to the early Fathers generally :—

'St. Paul, with his lines of thought striking their root deep into the religious thinking of Judaism [Hebraism ?], was a wholly closed book to these Gentile-Christian interpreters. If it is true that the questions which exercised the Apostle of the Gentiles had to a certain extent lost their immediate practical significance (for only the Jewish-Christian sects regarded the Mosaic law as still obligatory), at the same time

there was a complete drifting away from the connexion of St. Paul's
ideas with those of the Old Testament and the Judaism of his time. In
particular the purely moralizing view of things characteristic of these
Fathers, and the way in which they teach the freedom of the will, place
impassable barriers between them and the theology of St. Paul with its
purely religious premises, of which they have indeed no conception.
Law and the freedom of the Gospel, righteousness, faith, and election of
grace, all these root-ideas of the Pauline Epistles are either reduced to
common-places (verflacht) or filled with a wholly alien content. The
world of thought in which they moved was wholly different, and they
imported into primitive Christianity the conceptions of a wholly different civilization.' (*Inaugural Lecture*, delivered in 1871, and quoted by
Von Engelhardt, *Christenthum Justins des Märtyrers*, p. 59 f.)

In the concluding chapters of his work on the *Christianity
of Justin* (pp. 434–490) Von Engelhardt himself works out
at length the points which have just been summarized. He
shows clearly how the 'degeneration' in Justin's conception
of certain sides of Christian truth is due to his antecedents.
It was impossible that he should cast off the ideas in which
he had been brought up and which he had made his own
by earnest study, and that he should enter heart and soul
into modes of thought which had a wholly different history
and origin. All unconsciously a transfer took place : the
long list of terms and ideas which were handed on from
the Old Covenant to the New was retained, but their meaning was altered into conformity with the training and asso-
ciations of a Greek philosopher. And in this Justin's case
was only typical of what went on with the other leading
spirits among his contemporaries. Von Engelhardt does
well to insist upon this :—

'So in all directions Justin proves to be the key to the understanding
of the course which the Church took in its evolution. From his
writings alone can it be ascertained what is the origin of that peculiar
form of Christianity which meets us in different degrees in the Apostolic
Fathers ; and only through the analysis of the modes of his Christian
thinking can we get at the beginning of the so-called Old-Catholicism

and of the later Greek theology. The legal turn (Gesetzlichkeit) of Old-Catholic Christianity, the fluctuations of Ante-Nicene Christology and of the Logos-doctrine, and lastly the one-sided reference of σωτηρία or redemption to the imparting of eternal life in the sense of immortality, find their explanations in the confusion which is demonstrable in Justin of doctrines and ideas which are either specifically Christian or the products of Revelation generally with the religious and moral ideas of Greek and Pagan culture (des griechisch gebildeten Heidenthums).' (*Ibid.* p. 433 f.)

Harnack writes to the same general effect, only pointing out in addition the importance of the part played by the Jewish propaganda in preparing the way for this amalgamation of Greek thought with Christianity :—

'The conviction (that Christianity must possess all knowledge) soon had to be tested by its application to the Old Testament : that is to say, the greater number of thinking Christians had the problem set before them by the circumstances under which the Gospel had been preached to them of putting an intelligible meaning upon the Old Testament ; in other words, of using this Book as a Christian book, and of finding the means by which at once the Jews' claims upon it might be repelled, and their interpretation of it refuted. This problem would never have been raised, and still less would it have been solved, if the Christian communities in the Empire had not entered into the inheritance of the Jewish propaganda in which an extensive spiritualizing of the Old-Testament religion had already taken place. This spiritualizing was due to looking at the religion from the point of view of philosophy, and the tendency to look at it thus was the result of a prolonged action of Greek philosophy and the Greek spirit generally upon Judaism. It followed that all the facts and sayings of the Old Testament of which nothing could be made were converted into allegories. "Nothing was what it seemed, but it was only the symbol of something invisible. The narrative of the Old Testament was in this way sublimated into a history of the emancipation of Reason from Passion." It marks, however, the beginning of the world-wide development of Christianity, that it had to adopt the method of this fantastic syncretism as soon as it began to reflect upon itself or to apply and use the Book-Revelation which went with it. We have seen that the authors who made a diligent use of the Old Testament invariably employed the allegorical method. They were driven to this, not only by their inability to understand the literal sense of the Old Testament, or in other words by divergences of religious and moral opinion, but above all by the conviction that every page of that Book must speak of Christ and the Christian Church. How could such a conviction as this have seemed to be verified if the view of the Old Testament adopted by the current Jewish philosophy had not first effaced its definite concrete meaning?' (*Dogmengeschichte*, i. 187, ed. 2.)

A little further on Dr. Harnack remarks upon the pregnant significance of the fact that in order to hold its own at all the Old Testament had to have recourse 'to the allegorical method,' that is to a distinct section of Greek ideas, and that on the other hand it set up the strongest barrier to the complete Hellenizing of Christianity (*ibid.* p. 191 f.).

My last two quotations shall be taken from writers representing a different branch of theological study, no longer from historians of the Christian Church, but from students specially of the Old Testament. The first shall be from Ludwig Diestel, who wrote at an earlier date than any of the writers excerpted above except Ritschl, and in whom we shall therefore not be surprised at finding a less satisfactory explanation of the facts which he sets himself to account for, although he at least recognised clearly the receding of the Old Testament in the Post-Apostolic as compared with the Apostolic age, and the injury done to it by allegorical interpretation. The point which he misses is that with most of the writers of that date he sets down to Jewish influence what is due rather to Greek.

'In the lively controversy with Judaism and Jewish Christians the national and contemporary (zeitgeschichtliche) significance of the Old Testament retired more into the background; all that could not pass into the Christian faith as eternal truth found its explanation in Israel's sin. This controversy told disastrously on the conception of Christianity itself. The Apologists borrowed all the more readily from their opponents the identity of Covenant and Law, that the practical tendency of the first communities gave a great impulse to the conception of Christianity as a *nova lex*. Even in Pauline circles (Ep. Barn.) . . . the foundations of the theological conception were already laid when the Canon of the Old Testament was more sharply defined, and side by side with, or in the end above, it was placed the Canon of the New Covenant. The allegorical interpretation also for a long time contributed to its support in such a degree that the need for a theory of Hermeneutics which gradually made itself felt could only be satisfied by the better justification of this exegetical method. These powerful currents of interest with the controversies to right and left determine the formation of theological theory and the direction of Biblical studies in far higher degree than the recollections of the Apostolic age: the germs of what was best in these either lay neglected or else developed in a way that was extravagant and one-sided: the limitations imposed by the tendencies of the age which the Apostolic theory itself could not help admitting, were not gradually thrown off, but were rather in many respects accentuated, until at the end of the period knowledge sought new channels.' (*Geschichte d. A. T. in d. Christl. Kirche*, Jena, 1869, p. 17.)

The other passage is from a more recent writer, Dr. C. Siegfried, who brings us nearer to the problems of our own day. The expressive phrase in the first sentence has to be toned down somewhat in English.

'When one looks back over the history of the interpretation of the O. T., one gets the impression that the Church has been wholly incapable of assimilating it (als habe dasselbe der Kirche wie ein Stein im Magen gelegen). The book is as it were sealed with seven seals. One is reminded of Isa. xxix. 11, 12. Even he who could otherwise read well enough was hindered by the seals. The rest got no good from the book, because they could not read. Who was it then who so closed up the book? It was the Soferim and Perushim, the Scribes and Pharisees, when they made the end into the beginning, when they put the Torah first and so created the illusion which was to last for centuries that the Religion of Israel began with a Law. No one who starts from this assumption will ever come to understand the Old Testament. He who would really trace the development of the higher religion from the older popular religion of Israel must start from the Elder Prophets.'— (*Die theologische und die historische Betrachtung d. A. T.*, Frankfurt a. M., 1890, p. 26.)

From the Elder Prophets Dr. Siegfried recommends that the student should pass on to the Jehovistic document; from this to Deuteronomy, and then to Jeremiah and Deutero-Isaiah. That will bring him to the Exile, Ezekiel, and the Priestly Code. When he has felt the heavy yoke of the Law he will then be prepared to understand the light and easy yoke of Christ.

Probably the order thus sketched is the best that the student could adopt. By going first to Isaiah and the prophets who are grouped round him, he will penetrate at once to the very centre of the Religion of Israel: he will learn to understand its distinctive features: and he will be in the best position for tracing them both backwards in the order of their genesis and forwards in their ulterior developments.